SUFFERING

IS *NEVER* FOR

NOTHING

Other Works by Elisabeth Elliot

SUFFERING IS *NEVER* FOR NOTHING

ELISABETH ELLIOT

B&H
PUBLISHING
BRENTWOOD, TENNESSEE

978-1-5359-1415-4

Published by B&H Publishing Group
Brentwood, Tennessee

The publisher thanks Margaret.

Dewey Decimal Classification: 248.84
Subject Heading: FAITH / SUFFERING / DISCIPLESHIP

Scripture references marked KJV are taken from
the King James Version, public domain.

Scripture references marked NKJV are taken from
the New King James Version®. Copyright © 1982 by
Thomas Nelson. Used by permission. All rights reserved.

Scripture references marked NASB are taken from the New American
Standard Bible, copyright © 1960, 1962, 1963, 1968, 1971, 1972,
1973, 1975, 1977, 1995 by The Lockman Foundation.

Scripture references marked RSV are taken from the Revised Standard
Version, copyright © 1946, 1952, and 1971 the Division of Christian
Education of the National Council of the Churches of Christ in the
United States of America. Used by permission. All rights reserved.

Scripture references marked NIV are taken from the
New International Version, copyright ©1973, 1978, 1984, 2011 by
Biblica, Inc.® Used by permission. All rights reserved worldwide.

Scripture references marked NRSV are taken from the New Revised
Standard Version Bible, copyright © 1989 the Division of Christian
Education of the National Council of the Churches of Christ in the
United States of America. Used by permission. All rights reserved.
Vector leaf art courtesy of VectorStock.

8 9 10 11 12 • 28 27 26 25 24

Contents

Foreword

For centuries we've heard that the "blood of martyrs is the seed of the church," and the blood of Jim Elliot certainly overflowed the ink wells into which Elisabeth dipped her pen. She gave us invigorating *martyr-words* that inspired generations of courageous missionaries to take the gospel into foreboding jungles, deserts, and cities great and small. She also gave those same words to inspire us. Especially when suffering hit us broadside.

I was first introduced to Elisabeth Elliot in 1965 when, in high school, I read her book *Through Gates of Splendor*. I had no idea that right after graduation and a diving accident, I would enter those dark valleys about which Elisabeth wrote. I then met her years later in 1976 when we were both speakers at a conference in Canada. I was only twenty-six with less than a decade under my belt as a quadriplegic, and I could hardly believe I was sharing the same plenary platform with this saint of the age.

One evening, she came to my hotel room. As Elisabeth sat on the edge of my bed, we opened our hearts and shared how God had remained so faithful to us through so much suffering. We agreed that no one participates in God's joy without first tasting the afflictions of His Son. And before she left, she smiled and said, "Suffering is never for nothing, Joni." It was so Elisabethan, and I thought I understood what she meant. After all, nine years of quadriplegia had made me take seriously the lordship of Christ in my life, refining my faith, and giving me a deeper interest in prayer and the Word.

Two years later, I even wrote about these things in a book. I was pleased with my list of the thirty-five good biblical reasons as to why God allows affliction and what you can learn from it! I asked Elisabeth if she would offer an endorsement, which she did. But in her cover letter, she confessed that although the book was very satisfactory, it was a bit technical. Her comment crushed me. It took a few more years of quadriplegia, and the encroachment of chronic pain to help me see there was more—much more—to suffering than learning its theological background and benefits.

Elisabeth Elliot knew that true maturity, joy, and contentment has less to do with a mechanistic assessment of God's plan, and more to do with being pushed and, at times shoved, against the breast of your Savior. Not a tidy, orderly list, but an earnest grappling with the angel of the Lord. When affliction decimates you, then you understand Elisabeth's doctrine: The Bible's answers are never to be separated from the God of the Bible. That rich truth then guided me through more than fifty years of paralysis, pain, and cancer.

We are invigorated by Elisabeth's no-nonsense, go-out-and-die way of living the Christian life. She made us see that we are on a fierce battlefield upon which the mightiest forces of the universe converge in warfare. And we happily rise to that challenge, totally energized by this remarkable woman's exalted vision for the church. Her life and writings are food and drink to those whom God places upon altars of affliction.

And now with *Suffering Is Never for Nothing*, we have another collection of fresh, insightful writings from which to be nourished. Thankfully, although our friend is now in heaven, more of her material is now available to spur us on in the battle. The book you hold in your hands is a wonderful new portfolio of Elisabeth's ponderings, and as you peruse each page, imagine Elisabeth looking over your shoulder from the grandstands of heaven, encouraging you to embrace the Lord Jesus in *your* afflictions.

Let our friend show you how suffering is *never* for nothing. Linger long on this woman's sage wisdom, for there are epiphanies yet to dawn on your horizon, showing you even brighter excellencies of Jesus and more astounding beauties of His gospel. Let the timeless truths in this brand new book spur *you* on. Take to heart her words and one day when together we pass through heaven's gates, they will indeed be *splendorous*.

Joni Eareckson Tada
Joni and Friends International Disability Center
Spring 2019

Publisher's Preface

Elisabeth Elliot died on June 15, 2015 at her home in Magnolia, Massachusetts. At the time of her death, she had suffered dementia for many years and was undoubtedly ready to go be with the Savior of whom she taught so many so faithfully. I know that she did this because she taught me. I didn't have the opportunity to meet her until late in her life, when dementia had already stolen her voice, but her words will always be seared in my heart and mind.

> Hear the call of God to be a woman. Obey that call. Turn your energies to service. Whether your service is to be to a husband and through him and the family and home God gives you to serve the world, or whether you should remain, in the providence of God, single in order to serve the world without the solace of husband, home, and family, you will know fullness of life, fullness of liberty, and (I know whereof I speak) fullness of joy.

That quote, from *Let Me Be a Woman*, is one of hundreds that have challenged, encouraged, frustrated, and led me in my walk with God. Having not grown up in the church, I didn't learn of Elisabeth Elliot until she was already in declining health and had stopped publishing and recording her radio program. I was first exposed to her ministry in *Through Gates of Splendor* and I was quickly hooked on her writing.

Years later, as a publisher, I met a close friend of Elisabeth's. This friend had been discipled by Elisabeth for several years and a deep friendship had developed prior to her illness. This friend knew that I had been shaped by her books and had consumed all the teaching content I could find, so she sent me a gift that has borne much fruit. It was a set of six CDs that were called "Suffering Is Not for Nothing." I listened to these CDs and was amazed. Not only was it, I thought, perhaps her best content ever, it was some of the best teaching content I'd ever heard from anyone. I was able to get some additional copies of the CDs, which I gave to several close friends as gifts, and they all raved about the influence of the content on their lives as well.

Years went by, and I never stopped thinking about the clarity of the teaching on suffering that I had heard on those CDs. I just knew that the content would make an incredible book. Then in 2012, I had the opportunity to travel with our mutual friend who had given me the CDs, Elisabeth, and her husband, Lars Gren, to some events in Texas.

Elisabeth was in poor health and unable to communicate verbally. But there would be moments in which I could see the clarity of those piercing blue eyes connect with mine, she would grip my hand, try to speak, and I knew that she was in there understanding. I told her how God had used her in my life, and in the lives of hundreds of thousands of young women who would never have the privilege to tell her as I was then. At one point I found myself filled with anger toward God as I watched her struggle, trying to communicate. I couldn't understand how He would allow this incredible woman who had given Him so much to suffer in this way.

And then I heard her voice in my head say, "The cross is the gateway to joy." And was there any greater suffering than on the cross? I realized that the suffering I was observing was in no way inconsistent with the message she taught her entire life. She suffered much, and she always taught us through it. She finished well because she lived well.

It will be more than six years after that trip with her and nearly four years after her death when this book is published. It is a very slight adaptation of that set of CDs that I received many years ago. Never before published in book form, this material was originally delivered by Elisabeth at a small conference over the course of six sessions. I have edited only that content which will allow you, as a book reader, to not be distracted by references to "sessions," "yesterday's lesson," or things such as temporal references that have now shifted. It has been my effort to retain the distinct, clear voice of a woman and a writer.

It is my prayer that this book will re-introduce the work of Elisabeth Elliot to a new generation, while continuing to deepen the seeds she has already planted for so many of us.

Finally, re-reading this, I feel she would not appreciate all this adoration for her, so I must acknowledge that Elisabeth Elliot, although gifted and faithful, was a woman like any other. She was imperfect, a sinner, and was quick to admit it. What was extraordinary about her was the light of Christ that showed through all the cracks created in her by the extraordinary experiences she suffered.

But it was never for nothing.

Jennifer Lyell
October 2018

Chapter 1

The Terrible Truth

When I was told that my first husband, Jim, was missing in Auca Indian country, the Lord brought to my mind some words from the Prophet Isaiah "When thou passest through the waters, I will be with thee; and through the rivers, they shall not overflow thee" (Isa. 43:2 KJV). I prayed silently, Lord, let not the waters overflow. And He heard me and He answered me.

Two years later I went to live with the Indians who had killed Jim. Sixteen years after that, after I had come back to the states, I married a theologian named Addison Leitch. He died of cancer three and a half years later.

There have been some hard things in my life, of course, as there have been in yours, and I cannot say to you, I know exactly what you're going through. But I can say that I know the One who knows. And I've come to see that it's through the deepest suffering that God has taught me the deepest lessons. And if we'll trust Him for it, we can come through to the unshakable assurance that He's in charge. He has a loving purpose. And He can transform something terrible into something wonderful. Suffering is never for nothing.

When C. S. Lewis was asked to write a book on the problem of pain, he asked permission to write it anonymously. Permission was denied as not being in keeping with that particular series. And this is what he wrote in his preface, "If I were to say what I really thought about pain, I should be forced to make statements of such apparent fortitude that they would become ridiculous if anyone knew who made them."[1] I echo those sentiments.

There have been some hard things in my life, of course, as there have been in yours, and I cannot say to you, I know exactly what you're going through. But I can say that I know the One who knows. And I've come to see that it's through the deepest suffering that God has taught me the deepest lessons.

When I hear other people's stories about their own sufferings, I feel as though I know practically nothing about the subject myself. I'm in kindergarten, as it were, compared to, for example, my friend Jan who is a quadriplegic and lies on one side or the other twenty-four hours a day in a nursing home in Connecticut. Or my friend Judy Squires in California who was born with no legs. Or my late friend Joe Bayley, who lost three children.

But if all I knew about suffering was by observation alone, it would still be sufficient to tell me that we're up against a tremendous mystery. Suffering is a mystery that none of us is really capable of plumbing. And it's a mystery about which I'm sure everyone at some time or other has asked why. If we try to put together the mystery of suffering with the Christian idea of a God who we know loves us, if we think about it for as much as five minutes, the notion of a loving God cannot be possibly be deduced from the evidence that we see around us, let alone from human experience.

I'd like to go back to some of my own home training. I grew up in a very strong Christian home in Philadelphia where both of my parents were what I call seven-day-a-week kind of Christians. We had a little brass plate over the front doorbell that said "Christ is the head of this home, the unseen guest at every meal, the silent listener to every conversation." We were taught that God is love. I suppose one of the earliest hymns we were taught was that little gospel song, "Jesus loves me, this I know, for the Bible tells me so."

When I was nine years old, I lived in a neighborhood of forty-two boys, but I had a friend who lived about six blocks away whose name was Essie. And Essie and I were both nine years old when she died. When I was probably three or four years old, we had a guest in our home who was on her way to China as a missionary. Her name was Betty Scott. She went to China and married her fiancé John Stam. A few years later, I'm not sure just how old I was, maybe six or seven, my father came home one evening with a newspaper telling that John and Betty Stam had been captured by Chinese communists, marched almost naked through the streets of a Chinese village, and had then been beheaded.

You can imagine the impression this made on the mind of a young child in view of the fact that Betty Stam had sat at our supper table and had given us her testimony as she was on her way to China. I also remember very vividly the newspaper stories of the kidnapping of Charles Lindbergh's baby, and I would go to sleep at night imagining that I saw a ladder coming up by my window. And my parents, not knowing that I was concerned in this way, didn't think to tell me that there wasn't really a whole lot of danger that anybody was going to be interested in kidnapping a child like me because we were not really what you might call rich.

Nevertheless, I did have some experience of death as a small child. And just a few weeks ago, to bring it more up-to-date, some friends of my husband's and mine called to say that their little four-year-old child, who was born with spina bifida, was doing very well. But the mother was pregnant and for various reasons had had some tests which had revealed that the child she's now carrying also has spina bifida. And so they were calling just to say we're hurting. Please pray for us. And when I hear stories like that, it's what makes me think that my own experience of suffering is really very little.

The question is unavoidable for a thinking person. Where is God in all of this? Can you look at the data and believe? And it's the question that was put to Alyosha by Ivan Karamazov in Dostoevsky's famous novel, *The Brothers Karamazov*, recounting the story of a little girl of five.

Ivan said to his brother, Alyosha:

4

These educated parents subjected the poor five-year-old girl to every possible torture. They beat her, flogged her, kicked her, not knowing why themselves, until her whole body was nothing but bruises; all night in the outhouse, because she wouldn't ask to get up and go in the middle of the night (as if a five-year-old child sleeping its sound angelic sleep could have learned to ask by that age)—for that they smeared her face with her excrement and made her eat the excrement, and it was her mother, her mother who made her! And this mother could sleep while her poor child was moaning all night in that vile place! Can you understand that a small creature, who cannot even comprehend what is being done to her, in a vile place, in the dark and the cold, beats herself on her strained little chest with her tiny fist and weeps with her anguished, gentle, meek tears for "dear God" to protect her—can you understand such nonsense, my friend and my brother, my godly and humble novice, can you understand why this nonsense is needed and created? . . . And therefore I hasten to return my ticket. And it is my duty, if only as an honest man, to return it as far ahead of time as possible. Which is what I am doing. It's not that I don't accept God, Alyosha, I just

most respectfully return him the ticket . . .
Tell me straight out, I call on you—answer
me: imagine that you yourself are building
the edifice of human destiny with the object
of making people happy in the finale, of giving them peace and rest at last, but for that
you must inevitably and unavoidably torture
just one tiny creature, that same child who
was beating her chest with her little fist, and
raise your edifice on the foundation of her
unrequited tears—would you agree to be the
architect on such conditions? Tell me the
truth.[2]

And what I want to share with you is what I see to be the
straight truth with no evasions and no clear, flat platitudes.
It's very fresh in my mind just this week, a picture that I saw
in *Time* magazine of an inconsolable newborn baby whose
mother was on crack cocaine. Just to look at that picture
brought down on my own head, as it were, everything I was
planning to say to you in this series.

I happened to be sitting on the plane yesterday next
to a woman who was reading a book called *Master of Life
Manual*, which according to the cover was about metaphys-
ics, brain-mind awareness, human potential principles and
this stunning statement: "Create your own reality now." And
I thought I would hate to be down to such an extreme that I
had to create my own reality in the face of the data of human
experience.

So I would ask the question, is there a reason to believe that suffering is not for nothing? Is there an eternal and perfectly loving purpose behind it all? If there is, it's not obvious. It doesn't exactly meet the eye. Yet if for thousands of years in the face of these stunning realities—this terrible truth—people have believed that there is a loving God and that God is looking down on the realities around us and still loves us. If these people have still continued to insist that God knows what He's doing, that He's got the whole world in His hands, then I repeat, the reason cannot possibly be obvious. It can't be because those thousands of people were all deaf, dumb, blind, or stupid and incapable of looking clearly and steadily at the data that you and I are constantly having to look at. What is the answer?

F. W. H. Myers, in his poem *St. Paul*, wrote these words: "Is there not wrong too bitter for atoning? What are these desperate and hidden years? Hast Thou not heard Thy whole creation groaning, sighs of the bondsmen and a woman's tears?"[3] The answer is not obvious. There must be an explanation somewhere. And it's my purpose to try to get at the explanation and then to see if there's something that you and I can do about this question of suffering. I'm convinced that there are a good many things in this life that we really can't do anything about, but

> *I'm convinced that there are a good many things in this life that we really can't do anything about, but that God wants us to do something with.*

that God wants us to do something with. And I hope that by the time I'm finished, I will have made myself clear.

Now the word *suffering* may seem very high flowing and perhaps much too dignified for our particular set of troubles today. And I can look around this audience to whom I'm teaching this content and I don't know a person here, I have no idea who might receive this content later on in some other form. But if I knew you and if I knew your stories, then I would know that I can't possibly speak personally to every need that's here, to every kind of suffering. And I'm fairly sure that there would be some people here tonight that would be saying, well, I really don't know any such thing as suffering. I've never been through anything like Joni Eareckson or Jo Bailey or even Elisabeth Elliot, and of course, that's true. And I can say the very same thing if I knew your story. I could say, well, I've never been through anything like that.

So I want to give you a definition of suffering which will cover the whole gamut from when the washing machine overflows or when the roast burns and you're having the boss for dinner that night, all those things about which our immediate human reaction is oh, no! From that kind of triviality, relatively speaking, to your husband has cancer. Your child has spina bifida or you, yourself, have just lost everything. I think you'll find that the definition that I'm going to give you will cover that gamut.

The things that I'm going to try to say to you will apply to the small things, those sometimes ridiculously small things, that if you're anything like me, you get all upset about and all bent out of shape about, that matter not at all by comparison with the big things. And here it is, my definition of suffering. "Suffering is having what you don't want or wanting what you don't have." I think that covers everything.

Now can you imagine a world, for example, in which nobody had anything that he didn't want—no toothaches, no taxes, no touchy relatives, no traffic jams? Or by contrast, can you imagine a world in which everybody had everything they wanted—perfect weather, perfect wife, perfect husband, perfect health, perfect score, perfect happiness?

Malcolm Muggeridge said, "Supposing you eliminated suffering, what a dreadful place the world would be because everything that corrects the tendency of man to feel over-important and over-pleased with himself would disappear. He's bad enough now, but he would be absolutely intolerable if he never suffered."[4] Muggeridge gets at the heart of what I want to say. It's never for nothing.

Now how do I know that? The deepest things that I have learned in my own life have come from the deepest suffering. And out of the deepest waters and the hottest fires have come the deepest things that I know about God. And I imagine that most of you would say exactly the same. And I would add this, that the greatest gifts of my life have also entailed the greatest suffering. The greatest gifts of my life, for example, have been marriage and motherhood. And let's never forget that if we don't ever want to suffer, we must be very careful never to love anything or anybody. The gifts of love have been the gifts of suffering. Those two things are inseparable.

Now I come to you not like R. C. Sproul who is a theologian and a scholar. I come to you not merely as one who has stood on the sidelines and pondered these things, but as one in whose life God has seen to it that there has been a certain measure of suffering, a certain measure of pain. And it has been out of that very measure of pain that has come the unshakable conviction that God is love.

> *The deepest things that I have learned in my own life have come from the deepest suffering. And out of the deepest waters and the hottest fires have come the deepest things that I know about God.*

Now when my little girl, Valerie, was two years old, her father had been dead for more than a year. And I was beginning to teach her things like Psalm 23. "The LORD is my shepherd; I shall not want. He maketh me to lie down in green pastures: he leadeth me beside the still waters. He restoreth my soul" (Ps. 23:1–3a KJV). And I can still hear that tiny, little baby voice saying, "He leadeth me beside the still waters." And I realized when I heard her say that again—and I still have a tape of her saying that—I thought where did she get that weird intonation? And I realized that she got it from her mother who was coaching her word by word. She'd say, "He leadeth me," and I would say, "Beside." And she would say, "Beside." Anyway, she learned it.

And things like Psalm 91, one of my favorite psalms, "He that dwelleth in the secret place of the most High shall abide under the shadow of the Almighty. I will say of the LORD, He is my refuge and my fortress: my God; in him will I trust. Surely he shall deliver thee from the snare of the fowler, and from the noisome pestilence. He shall cover thee with his feathers, and under his wings shalt thou trust: his truth shall be thy shield and buckler. Thou shalt not be afraid for the terror by night; nor for the arrow that flieth by day; Nor for the pestilence that walketh in darkness; nor for the destruction that wasteth at noonday. A thousand shall fall at thy side, and ten thousand at thy right hand; but it shall not come nigh thee" (Ps. 91:1–7 KJV).

The greatest gifts of my life have also entailed the greatest suffering.

Now I want you to think of how a mother, who is a widow, tries to teach her little daughter whose father was killed by a group of savage Indians who thought that he was a cannibal what this psalm means. What the words of Scripture mean. She learned "Jesus loves me, this I know," not because her daddy was killed. She didn't know it that way. But rather, "Jesus loves me this I know, for *the Bible* tells me so." She learned to sing "God will take care of me," and how was I to explain a thousand shall fall at thy side and ten thousand at thy right hand but it shall not come nigh thee?

I tell you this because maybe it'll help you to see that I've been forced, from the circumstances in my own life, to try to get down to the very bedrock of faith. The things that are infrangible and unshakable. God is my refuge. Was He Jim's refuge? Was He his fortress? On the night before those five men who were killed by the Waorani went into the Waorani territory they sang, "We rest on thee, our Shield and our Defender." What does your faith do with the irony of those words?

There would be no intellectual satisfaction on this side of Heaven to that age-old question, why. Although I have not found intellectual satisfaction, I have found peace. The answer I say to you is not an explanation but a person, Jesus Christ, my Lord and my God. As I shared at the beginning of this chapter, when I came to the realization that my husband was missing, not knowing for another five days that he was dead, the words that God brought to me then were from Isaiah the 43rd chapter, "When thou passest through the waters I will be with thee; and through the rivers, they shall not overflow thee: when thou walkest through the fire, thou shalt not be burned; neither shall the flame kindle upon thee. For I am the LORD thy God" (Isa. 43:2–3a KJV).

And I realized then that God was not telling me that everything was going to be fine, humanly speaking, that He was going to preserve my husband physically and bring him back to me. But He was giving me one unmistakable promise: I will be with you. For I am the Lord your God. He is the one who loved me and gave Himself for me.

And that challenge that Ivan Karamazov gave to his brother, Alyosha, echoed a challenge that was given thousands of years earlier, the challenge flung at Jesus when He hung on the cross. You who would destroy the temple and build it in three days, save yourself. If you're the Son of God, come down. And then you remember how the religious elite in derision taunted Him with words that accused. *He saved others. Himself, He could not save. He trusts in God. Let God deliver Him now. He's a miracle worker. Let Him prove it to us now because He said I am the Son of God.*

And so, we come back again to the terrible truth that there is suffering. The question remains, is God paying attention? If so, why doesn't He do something? I say He has, He did, He is doing something, and He will do something.

The subject can only be approached by the cross. That old, rugged cross so despised by the world. The very worst thing that ever happened in human history turns out to be the very best thing because it saved me. It saves the world. And so God's love, which was represented, demonstrated to us in His giving His Son Jesus to die on the cross, has been brought together in harmony with suffering.

You see, this is the crux of the question. And those of you who have studied Latin may remember that the word *crux* is the Latin word, *crux*, for cross. It's only in the cross that we can begin to harmonize this seeming contradiction between suffering and love. And

The gifts of love have been the gifts of suffering. Those two things are inseparable.

we will never understand suffering unless we understand the love of God.

We're talking about two different levels on which things are to be understood. And again and again in the Scriptures we have what seem to be complete paradoxes because we're talking about two different kingdoms. We're talking about this visible world and an invisible Kingdom on which the facts of this world are interpreted.

Take for example the Beatitudes, those wonderful statements of paradox that Jesus gave to the multitudes when He was preaching to them on the mountain. And He said very strange things like this: How happy are those who know what sorrow means. Happy are those who claim nothing. Happy are those who have suffered persecution. What happiness will be yours when people blame you and ill treat you and say all kinds of slanderous things against you. Be glad then, yes, be tremendously glad.

Does it make any sense at all? Not unless you see that there are two kingdoms: the kingdom of this world, and the kingdom of an invisible world. And the apostle Paul understood the difference when he made this stunning declaration. He said it is now my happiness to suffer for You, my happiness to suffer. It sounds like nonsense, doesn't it? And yet this is the Word of God. Janet Erskine Stuart said, "Joy is not the absence of suffering but the presence of God."[5]

It's what the psalmist found in the valley of the shadow of death. You remember, he said, "I will fear no evil." Now the psalmist was not naïve enough to say I will fear no evil because there isn't any. There is. We live in an evil, broken, twisted, fallen, distorted world. What did he say? "I will fear no evil; for thou art with me; thy rod and thy staff they comfort me."

And when I stood by my shortwave radio in the jungle of Ecuador in 1956 and heard that my husband was missing, and God brought to my mind the words of the Prophet Isaiah, "When thou passest through the waters, I will be with thee." You can imagine that my response was not terribly spiritual. I was saying, but Lord, You're with me all the time. What I want is Jim. I want my husband. We had been married twenty-seven months after waiting five and a half years.

Five days later I knew that Jim was dead. And God's presence with me was not Jim's presence. That was a terrible fact. God's presence did not change the terrible fact that I was a widow and I expected to be a widow until I died because I thought it was a miracle I got married the first time. I couldn't imagine that I would ever get married a second time, let alone a third time. God's presence did not change the fact of my widowhood. Jim's absence thrust me, forced me, hurried me to God, my hope and my only refuge.

And I learned in that experience who God is. Who He is in a way that I could never have known otherwise. And so I can say to you that suffering is an irreplaceable medium through which I learned an indispensable truth. I Am. I am the Lord. In other words, that God is God. Well, I still want to go back and say, but Lord, what about those babies? What about that little child with spina bifida? What about those babies born terribly handicapped, with terrible suffering because their mothers were on cocaine or heroin or alcohol? What about my little Scottie dog, McDuff, who died of cancer at the age of six? What about the Lindbergh baby and the Stams who were beheaded? What about all of that?

And I can't answer your questions, or even my own, except in the words of Scripture, these words from the apostle Paul who knew the power of the cross of Jesus. And this is what he wrote: "For I reckon that the sufferings of this present time are not worthy to be compared with the glory which shall be revealed in us. For the earnest expectation of the creature waiteth for the manifestation of the sons of God" (Rom. 8:18–19 KJV). It was made the victim of frustration—all those animals, all those babies who have no guilt whatsoever—the victim of frustration, not by its own choice, but because of him who made it so; yet always there was hope. And this is the part that brings me immeasurable comfort: The universe itself is to be freed from the shackles of mortality and enter upon the liberty and splendor of the children of God.

Where does this idea of a loving God come from? It is not a deduction. It is not man so desperately wanting a god that he manufactures Him in his mind. It's He who was the Word before the foundation of the world, suffering as a lamb slain. And He has a lot up His sleeve that you and I haven't the slightest idea about now. He's told us enough so that we know that suffering is never for nothing.

Suffering is an irreplaceable medium through which I learned an indispensable truth.

Chapter 2

The Message

I look upon suffering as one of God's ways of getting our attention. In fact, C. S. Lewis said, "God whispers to us in our pleasures, speaks in our conscience, but shouts in our pain: it is His megaphone to rouse a deaf world."[6] I'd like for us to think about some of the things that God needs to say to us, for which He needs to get our attention. First of all, it's interesting to me, it's of great significance, that as far as we know the oldest book in the Bible is the book of Job. Of all the books in the Bible, it is this one that deals most specifically and head-on with the subject of suffering. You may recall that Job was called a blameless man, a righteous man. God, Himself, said that Job was a blameless man. This is significant because the common understanding of morality those days was that a good man would be blessed and an evil man would be punished . . . so, Job's experience seemed to turn that completely upside-down.

Job lost everything. His ten children were killed in a storm. His vast number of animals were killed. His household was essentially destroyed. This man who had been esteemed, wealthy by all accounts, was without all that signified wealth and blessing. Yet the destruction did not stop there. His physical body suffered as well with painful boils and disfigurement so significant that he was unrecognizable to some of his closest friends. All of this happened and Job did not know why. You may remember that there was a drama that went on behind the scenes that, as far as we know, Job was never given a clue about, where Satan challenged God in Heaven. And he said, of course Job trusts You. But does he trust You for nothing? Try taking away all those blessings and then see where Job's faith goes. And God accepted Satan's challenge. And here we have a mystery that we cannot begin to explain. In fact, it was God who called Satan's attention to that individual, Job. And He gave Satan permission to take things away from Job.

And so he lost his flocks and his herds and his servants and his sons and his daughters and his house and finally even the confidence of his wife. And as he sat on his ash heap and his health had been touched by that time and he was scraping himself with potsherds and in utter anguish and misery, he kept silent for seven days as his friends—as they were called and had apparently been when times were good—sat there and looked at him and didn't say anything either for seven days. And when Job finally broke silence, he howled his complaints at God.

We may often hear Job called a patient man but if you read the book of Job you won't really find a lot of evidence that he was patient. But he never doubted that God existed and he said some of the very worst things that could possibly be said about God. And isn't it interesting that the Spirit of God preserved those things for you and me? God is big enough to take anything that we can dish out to Him. And He even saw to it that Job's howls and complaints were preserved in black and white for our instruction. So never hesitate to say what you really feel to God because remember that God knows what you think before you know and certainly knows what you're going to say before you even think it.

So for some samples of these dreadful things that this patient man, Job, said to God, how about Job chapter 3, verses 11, 19, and 20 where he says why was I not stillborn? Why did I not die when I came out of the womb? Why should the sufferer be born to see the light? Why is life given to men who find it so bitter?

You see Job here dialoguing with God. There is no question in Job's mind throughout this entire book of the existence of God. He knows that it is God with whom he has to reconcile his circumstances. Somebody is behind all this, he's saying. And the question "why" presupposes that there is reason, that there is a mind behind all that may appear to be mindless suffering. We would never ask the question why if we really believed that the whole of the universe was an accident and that you and I are completely at the mercy of chance. The very question why, even if it is flung at us by one who calls himself an unbeliever or an atheist is a dead give-away that there is that sneaking suspicion in the back of every human mind that there is somebody, some reason, some thinking individual behind this.

And then in Job chapter 10, Job addresses God directly. And he says can't You take Your eyes off me? Won't You leave me alone long enough to swallow my spit? You shaped me and made me; now You've turned to destroy me. You kneaded me like clay, and now You're grinding me to a powder. Anybody ever felt like that? Does that ring any bells out there? God is grinding me to a powder. He doesn't even give me a chance to swallow my spit.

> We would never ask the question why if we really believed that the whole of the universe was an accident and that you and I are completely at the mercy of chance.

But what about his friends? His friends who were very religious. Well, they never say a word that is not theologically sound as they understand the ways of God. They begin to accuse him of foolish notions, a belly full of wind, they say. Job is utterly lacking in the fear of God and he is pitting himself against the Almighty, charging Him head down like an angry bull.

When Job calls Eliphaz a windbag, this is, you know, the pot calling the kettle black. But his friends and enemies, he says, can't hold a candle to God who "has shattered me; He also has taken me by my neck, and shaken me to pieces; He has set me up for His target, His archers surround me. He pierces my heart and does not pity; He pours out my gall on the ground" (Job 16:12–13 NKJV). Now can you top that when you are railing at God for the broken heart borne out of suffering? Would you dare to say such things aloud?

And then Job asks God question after question after question. And at one point he says if I ask Him a thousand questions, He won't even answer one of them. And he was right. Remember that when God finally breaks His silence, God does not answer a single question. God's response to Job's questions is mystery. In other words, God answers Job's mystery with the mystery of Himself.

And He starts right in nailing poor Job with questions. Where were you when I laid the foundation of the world? Who laid the cornerstone when the morning stars sang together? Have you seen the treasures of the snow? Who enclosed the sea with doors? Have you walked in the great deep? Have you ever in your life commanded the morning and caused the dawn to know its place? Have you presided over the doe in labor? Tell me, where is the way to the dwelling of light? He goes on and on and on; question after question after question.

God answers Job's mystery with the mystery of Himself.

He knows the answers to these questions, of course. And he knows that Job most certainly cannot answer them. He is revealing to Job who He is. God, through my own troubles and sufferings, has not given me explanations. But He has met me as a person, as an individual, and that's what we need. Who of us in the worst pit that we've ever been in needs anything as much as we need company? Just somebody, perhaps, who will sit there in silence but just be with us. Job never denies God's existence, never imagines that God has nothing to do with his troubles, but he has a thousand questions and so do we.

⁂

Now, it may seem like an odd transition, but this is a good place for me to tell you a story or two that comes out of my first year as a missionary. I thought of myself as being very well prepared to be a missionary. As I said, I came from a strong Christian home. My parents had been missionaries themselves. And we had dozens, probably hundreds of missionaries traipsing through our house. We had a guest room that always seemed to be full. We had suitcases bumping up and down the stairs all the time. And we listened, from our earliest memories, to many, many missionary stories at our own dinner table.

Who of us in the worst pit that we've ever been in needs anything as much as we need company?

I went to a school for missionary's children, and I heard thousands of missionary talks. I looked at tens of thousands of terrible missionary slides showing pictures of church plants, baptisms, and Vacation Bible Schools all in grainy, generally indistinguishable portrayal. I lived, ate, breathed, drank missionaries and turned out to be a missionary myself, as were four of my other brothers and sister. There were six of us in the family. Five of us turned out to be missionaries of one sort or another, and the sixth is a professor in a Christian college.

I thought that I was probably God's gift to the mission field as a missionary and had all this training behind me. I went to a Bible School and I had some Home Missionary work in Canadian Sunday School Mission. I mean, I had it all. But within the first year God saw fit to give me three major blows to what I thought was a very well-founded and boldly developed faith.

The first of these blows came as I was attempting to learn an unwritten Indian language in the western jungle of Ecuador, the language of the Colorado Tribe. They were a very small tribe who had never had any written language and therefore had none of the Bible in their language. I had prayed that God would give me an informant, someone who would be prepared to sit down with me and go over and over and over what for him was the easiest language in the world. I knew this informant would need to have the patience to deal with this apparently ignorant foreigner.

And God answered my prayer by sending me this man by the name of Macadao who was bilingual, which was an enormous advantage. He spoke Spanish and Colorado. This was significant as I had already learned Spanish as the national language of the country. We worked together very happily for about two months. Then, I was on my knees one morning in my bedroom, as was my habit, reading my Bible and praying. And I happened to be reading in the third chapter or the fourth chapter of 1 Peter. And these were the words: "Think it not strange concerning the fiery trial which is to try you, as though some strange thing happened unto you" (1 Pet. 4:12 KJV). And at that very point I heard gunshots.

There was nothing unusual about gunshots in that particular clearing of the jungle. We were surrounded by Indians who hunted with guns that they had bought from the white man. And there were white people also in that clearing who hunted as well. So we often heard gunshots. But these particular gunshots were followed by yelling and screaming and horses galloping and people running and general pandemonium.

So I rushed outside to hear that Macadao had just been murdered. Now it would be very nice if I could tell you that I easily found another informant. But the truth was that Macadao was literally the only person in the world who was capable of doing the job that he had been doing with me. Nobody else knew both Spanish and Colorado.

So I was faced, for the first time in my personal experience, with that awful why. Like Job, I didn't doubt for a second that God was up there, that God knew what He was doing. But I couldn't imagine what He could possibly have in mind. And God's answer to my why was "Trust Me." No explanations. Just, trust Me. That was the message.

Now if I had had a faith that was determined God had to give me a particular kind of answer to my particular prayers, that faith would have disintegrated. But my faith had to be founded on the character of God Himself. And so, what looked like a contradiction in terms: God loves me;

God lets this awful thing happen to me. What looked like a contradiction in terms, I had to leave in God's hands and say okay, Lord. I don't understand it. I don't like it. But I only had two choices. He is either God or He's not. I am either held in the Everlasting Arms or I'm at the mercy of chance and I have to trust Him or deny Him. Is there any middle ground? I don't think so.

I thought of Daniel in the lions' den. I remember the picture that we had on our wall at home, a painting. When I was a child I often gazed at that painting. And Daniel is standing in the den of lions. There's a light on his face and he stands very tall and straight with his hands behind his back. And just very faintly in the dark you can see these glowing eyes of the hungry lions.

I am either held in the Everlasting Arms or I'm at the mercy of chance and I have to trust Him or deny Him

And I realized that the painting is telling me that here's a man whose faith rests in the character of God. Now of course, I wouldn't have put it in those terms as a child. But that picture spoke volumes to me. God was there in the pit. He was not making it unnecessary for Daniel to go into the pit anymore than it was unnecessary for Joseph to go into that pit where his jealous brothers threw him or to be put into prison, as were Paul and Silas and Peter and many other people in Scripture, even John the Baptist who got his head chopped off.

It was necessary for Shadrach and Meshach and Abednego to go into the fiery furnace because God had a message not just for Shadrach, Meshach, and Abednego but also, you remember, for the king. He said "has your God, whom you serve, been able to deliver you?" And you remember his challenge before he threw them into the furnace, "Who is that God that shall deliver you out of my hands?" (Dan. 3:15 KJV). And, then come those ringing words of faith, "If it be so, our God whom we serve is able to deliver us from the burning fiery furnace, and he will deliver us out of thine hand, O king. But if not, be it known unto thee, O king, that we will not serve thy gods, nor worship the golden image which thou hast set up" (Dan. 3:17–18 KJV). But if not . . .

And that is the lesson that has to come to all of us in some point in our lives. Every one of us, I'm sure, sooner or later, has to face up to that painful question. Why? And God is saying, trust Me. If your prayers don't get answered the way you thought they were supposed to be, what happens to your faith? The world says God doesn't love you. The Scriptures tell me something very different. Those "blesseds" of the Beatitudes. Paul's word, it is my happiness to suffer for You.

> *If your prayers don't get answered the way you thought they were supposed to be, what happens to your faith? The world says God doesn't love you. The Scriptures tell me something very different.*

We don't know the answer. But we know it lies deep within the mystery of the freedom to choose. When God created man, Adam and Eve, He created them with the freedom to choose to love Him or to defy Him. And they chose to defy Him. Adam and Eve abused that freedom. And C. S. Lewis says in his book, *The Problem of Pain*, "Man is now a horror to God and to himself and a creature ill-adapted to the universe not because God made him so but because he has made himself so by the abuse of his free will."[7] And Lewis goes on to state this knotty problem in its simplest form. "If God were good, He would wish to make His creatures perfectly happy, and if God were almighty He would be able to do what He wished. But the creatures are not happy. Therefore, God lacks either goodness, or power, or both."[8]

So, answering the question depends upon our definition of good. An ancient man thought of goodness in moral terms. Modern man equates good with happiness. If it ain't fun, it ain't good. The two things almost seem to be mutually exclusive. They put it the other way around, if it's good, it ain't fun. There's a commercial I've seen recently for some kind of cereal with two little kids who have heard that it's natural and it's good for you. So they said, "Well let's get him to try it. He'll eat anything. He doesn't know it's good for you." So the little kid eats it because he doesn't know any better that the other two kids wouldn't try it because it's good for you. And perhaps you've heard the saying, "Everything that I like is either illegal, immoral, or fattening," a notion that the world has that the two things are mutually exclusive. If it's good, it's not fun. It has nothing to do with my happiness. Moral man was concerned primarily with moral goodness.

If we learn to know God in the midst of our pain, we come to know Him as one who is not a High Priest that cannot be touched with the feeling of our infirmities. He is one who has been over every inch of the road. I love that old hymn by Richard Baxter, "Christ leads me through no darker rooms than He went through before." I love those words.

I have some dear friends who are missionaries in North Africa. He was one of the many seminary students who have lived in our house. And I had a letter from them about a year or so ago to tell me that they had just lost their baby girl. I think it was either at birth or just within a few hours after birth. And their letter was filled with the anguish that that cost them. And of course, I wanted to answer the letter. But I've never lost a baby. I only have one child who was ten months old when her father was killed. And I so couldn't write to Phil and Janet and say I know exactly what you've been through. But I've read the wonderful letters of Samuel Rutherford, that Scottish preacher from the seventeenth century who seems to have been through just

If we learn to know God in the midst of our pain, we come to know Him as one who is not a High Priest that cannot be touched with the feeling of our infirmities. He is one who has been over every inch of the road.

about every imaginable human mill, and he had lost at least one child and I had his letter in my study.

And so I looked up one of his letters to a woman who had lost a child. And this is what he wrote to her, so I quoted these words to Phil and Janet after saying to them that I didn't know what you're going through but I know the One who knows, and then I sent them Samuel Rutherford's words. This is what he said after losing two daughters: "Grace rooteth not out the affections of a mother, but putteth them on His wheel who maketh all things new, that they may be refined . . . He commandeth you to weep: and that princely One, who took up to heaven with Him a man's heart to be a compassionate High Priest . . . The cup ye drink was at the lip of sweet Jesus, and He drank of it."

Janet wrote to me this reply, "The storm of pain is calming down and the Lord is painting a new and different picture of Himself."[9] I saw in her experience that the very suffering itself was an irreplaceable medium. God was using that thing to speak to Janet and Phil in a way that He could not have spoken if He had not gotten their attention through the death of that little child.

Now I don't mean to simplify, to over-simply things as though that explains it, that God had to say something to those two people because if I know anything about godliness I know that Phil and Janet Linton are both godly people. That raises another painful question, doesn't it? We often say why did such and such have to happen to her? She's such a wonderful person. Why did he have to go through this? He's such a wonderful person. Well, again, the word is, "Trust Me."

Back when I was a college student, I was dabbling around in poetry, as I suppose most teenage girls do at some point. I wrote some words that later on seemed to me to be almost prophetic. I wrote these words and I really don't remember exactly whether there was any particular reason why I wrote them at the time, but something had given me a clue that there could be some loneliness ahead for me. So these were the words that I wrote,

> Perhaps some future day, Lord, Thy strong
> hand will lead me
> to the place where I must stand
> utterly alone.
> Alone, O gracious lover, but for Thee.
> I shall be satisfied if I can see Jesus only.
> I do not know Thy plan for years to come,
> my spirit finds in
> Thee its perfect home.
> Sufficiency.
> Lord, all my desire is before Thee now, lead
> on no matter
> where, no matter how.
> I trust in Thee.

I began keeping journals back when I was about sixteen or seventeen, and I've been keeping them ever since. That makes quite a few years at this point. So I went back to re-read some of those earlier journals in preparation for this message. I thought, well, you know, I'd really better go back and see whether I know anything about what I'm talking about.

I found a few little things in the journal, despite my earlier admission that I don't think I know very much by comparison with others. And one of the things I noted that I did feel was significant was the fact that again and again I quote hymns about the cross, hymns which were favorites at different times. And one of them that I learned in college was, "O, teach me what it meaneth that Cross uplifted high, with one the man of sorrows condemned to bleed and die."[10] One of the hymns that we learned as very small children in our family prayers—we used to sing a hymn every morning in family prayers—was "Jesus Keep Me Near the Cross."[11]

My daughter has taught some of those hymns to her own children, and I don't think I will ever forget seeing little two-year-old Jim violently swinging his newborn baby sister, Colleen, in one of those little canvas swings and singing, "In the Cross, in the Cross, be my glory ever. Till my raptured soul shall find rest beyond the river." And here's this little boy, just violently swinging this infant who is having the time of her life and singing this profound hymn about the cross.

I could go on and on with hymns I could quote. "Beneath the Cross of Jesus" has always been a favorite of mine. But as I came across those in my journals, I thought, what did I imagine would be the answer to the prayers that I was praying in those hymns? What kind of an answer did

I really expect God to give me? Did I expect some kind of a miraculous revelation? Perhaps some deep original insight into the meaning of the cross? Did I expect God to make some kind of a spiritual giant out of me so that I would have mysteries at my fingertips about which other people didn't know anything? Well I haven't the slightest idea what I really thought. I supposed it was all very vague and mystical in my mind, and I didn't know what God would do by way of answering that prayer.

But I can look back over these forty-five years or so and see that God, in fact, is in the process of answering those prayers. Teach me what it means, that cross lifted up high. What is this great symbol of the Christian faith? It's a symbol of suffering. That is what the Christian faith is about. It deals head-on with this question of suffering, and no other religion in the world does that. Every other religion, in some way, evades the question. Christianity has, at its very heart, this question of suffering.

It comes, the answer to our prayers, teach me what it means, "In the cross be my glory ever." The answer comes not in the form of a revelation or an explanation or a vision but in the form of a person. He comes to you and me in our sorrow. And He says, "Trust Me." "Walk with Me."

I have to insert in here another little grandchild story and you're going have to bear with me. You know grandmothers do tell grandchild stories. But they seem so appropriate so often. And in this particular case, my little four-year-old granddaughter, Christiana, had to be spanked four times, three times in one day for the same offense. She had not come running quickly when she was called. And my daughter, just as my mother treated delayed obedience as disobedience, Valerie tries to do the same thing. And so Christiana was spanked three times on that particular Sunday.

So Sunday night when it was time to go to church and she was called, she came charging out to the car, tears pouring down her face, her arms full of a Bible, a notebook, a pen—four years old, mind you—on her way to church had to have a Bible, notebook, a pen, her barrettes, her necklaces, her bracelets, her hair ribbons, and who knows what else was essential. All this stuff falling out of her arms. She was tripping over things. Tears pouring down her face. And she stopped and she said, "Oh, momma. If only Adam and Eve hadn't sinned." Now that child was suffering because she lives in a fallen world and you and I live in that same fallen world.

We have to look at these awful facts, the fact of sin and suffering and death, the fact that God created a world in which those things were possible. The fact that He does love us, that means He wants nothing less than our perfection and joy. The fact that He gave us the freedom to choose and man decided that his own idea of perfection and joy was better than God's and believed what Satan told him, therefore sin and suffering entered into the world. And now we're saying, why doesn't God do something about it? And the Christian answer is, He did. He became the victim, a lamb slain from before the foundation of the world.

George Herbert, another seventeenth-century poet, wrote this, "Afflictions sorted, anguish of all sizes. Fine nets and schemes[12] to catch us in."[13] Then George MacDonald the nineteenth-century poet said this, "Pain, with dog and spear, false faith with human hearts will hunt and hound."[14] These give us two different expressions of what God is doing. Fine nets and schemes to catch us in, to give us this message. And, the second expression is reiterated as the psalmist said in Psalm 46, "God is our refuge and strength, a very present help in trouble. Though the earth be removed, and though the mountains be carried into the midst of the sea" (Ps. 46:1–2 kjv).

I speak to you as one who has desperately needed a refuge. And in that same Psalm he says, "be still." I'm told that it's legitimate to translate that, "shut up and know that I am God." That's the message.

He comes to you and me in our sorrow.
And He says, "Trust Me." "Walk with Me."

⚛ Chapter 3 ⚛

Acceptance

I want to tell you a little story that may offend some of you. I hope it will not be too offensive, but I have actually been accused, at times, of being frivolous about the fact that I've had two husbands who have died. So, I don't want to seem frivolous, but I'm sure you all realize that the subject of these talks is a very heavy one. And here's a story that does fit in very nicely under this particular heading.

An incident happened a couple of years ago. Lars and I were in Birmingham, Alabama. And it was a breakfast and Lars was setting up his book table. And there was a little lady there setting place cards out at the various tables. And he and she were chatting back and forth. There was no one else around at the time. And suddenly she turned to him and she said, "By the way," she said, "What's your name?" And he said, "Well," he said, "I'm an Elliott, too." And she looked at him and she said, "Are you the speaker's husband?" And he said, "Yes." And she said "Well, that's funny. They, I thought they told me you had a different name." And he said, "Well, I have actually. My name's Gren." But he said, "You know, I'm the third husband." And her face fell, and she said, "Oh my goodness, but we only have one place card." She was completely serious. And Lars said, "I don't think you need to worry. The other two are dead. I don't think they're going to show up."

Well now, how does that fit in with the subject of acceptance? Quite simply, I could not possibly talk this way about Jim and Ad if it hadn't been for the fact that by the grace of God I was enabled to accept their death. And people have come to me more than once in my life and said how can you possibly talk about your late husbands in that frivolous and flippant way? And I've even had some widows say to me, how do you keep from comparing your husbands? And I say I don't.

I've made all kinds of comparisons between my husbands. And you can be sure that I would never have accepted Lars's proposal if he didn't compare very favorably with the first two. Although they are very different men, at least they had one thing in common, and that was that they liked me. But the fact is that they're men with very different gifts. And one of the things which God brought to my mind when I was considering Lars's proposal before I'd given him an answer was a verse in 1 Corinthians 12. Men have different gifts but it's the same Lord who accomplishes His purposes through them all.

Acceptance, I believe, is the key to peace in this business of suffering. As I've said, the crux of the whole matter is the cross of Jesus Christ. And that word *crux* means *cross*. It is the best thing that ever happened in human history as well as the worst thing. Here in *His* love, the Scripture tells us. Not that we loved God here in His love, not that *we* loved God but that He loved us and gave Himself, no, here in *His* love that Christ laid down His life for us.

When we speak of love as the Bible speaks of love, we're not talking about a silly sentiment. We're not talking about a mood or a feeling or warm fuzzies. The love of God is not a sentiment. It is a willed and inexorable love that will command nothing less than the very best for us. The love of God wills our joy. I think of the love of God as being synonymous with the will of God.

> *Not that we loved God here in His love, not that we loved God but that He loved us and gave Himself, no, here in His love that Christ laid down His life for us.*

Young people sometimes say to me this whole business of the will of God is just so scary. I don't see how you can ever just turn over your whole life to God without knowing what He's going to do. Well, that's what faith is about, isn't it? If you really believe that somebody loves you then you trust them. The will of God is love. And love suffers. That's how we know what the love of God for us is, because He was willing to become a man and to take upon Himself our sins, our griefs, our sufferings.

Love is always inextricably bound with sacrifice. Any father knows this. Any mother knows this. You may have known it in theory but when that baby is born, if the mother has not suffered before that—during those nine months—certainly there comes the time when she has to suffer. And when that baby is born and the labor is over with, then we all, we mothers know that's just the beginning, isn't it? And no father or mother can possibly imagine what changes there will be in their lives, no matter how much they may have read and how much they may have observed. But the presence of that new little human being in their lives changes everything.

> The will of God is love.
> And love suffers.

And it's sacrifice, day in and day out, night in and night out. But it's not something about which you sit down and feel sorry for yourself. It's not something you moan and groan about, except perhaps once in a while. But it *is* very real, isn't it? It is my life for yours. And that, ladies and gentlemen, is the principle of the cross. That's what Jesus was demonstrating. My life for yours.

Suffering is a mystery. It is not explained, but it is affirmed. And we must remember that all of Christianity rests on mysteries. Those of you who belong to churches that use creeds know that you are articulating a set of statements about the faith, every one of which deals with a mystery. Is there anyone who calls himself a Christian that can explain the Trinity? Is there anyone who can get at the gynecology, for example, of the virgin birth? Is there any specialist in aerodynamics that could tell us anything about the Ascension? These are mysteries. Creation, Redemption, Incarnation, Crucifixion, Resurrection—these great key words of the Christian faith are mysteries.

We stand up as a body in church—the church that I go to, for example—and we say a creed out loud together. We are not explaining anything. We are simply affirming. And that's what Christianity is about. God is God. God is a three-personed God. He loves us. We are not adrift in chaos. To me that is the most fortifying, the most stabilizing, the most peace-giving thing that I know anything about in the universe. Every time things have seemingly fallen apart in my

Suffering is a mystery. It is not explained, but it is affirmed. And we must remember that all of Christianity rests on mysteries.

life, I have gone back to those things that do not change. Nothing in the universe can ever change those facts. He loves me. I am not at the mercy of chance.

Lars and I got to the airport once for a flight to some place or other, and I think our flight was supposed be at 11:30 in the morning. We got there about 10:30 and, lo and behold, the airport was closed. There were lines all the way from the ticket counters out to the sidewalk. You couldn't even get through the revolving doors into the airport in Boston. We were told that all flights had been cancelled, that the airlines were taking no responsibility for rebooking for anything. You had to get in line and start over. To top it off, your tickets would mean nothing as far as bookings were concerned. It was a scene of real horror and chaos. People were crying, people were angry, people were despondent. It was a mess. I felt so sorry for those families that had little children and they were headed for Orlando to go to Disney World for their winter break, and college students with skis.

But there were fist-fights. There were people so angry with the poor ticket agents that they were actually coming to blows. And we heard that there was one planeload of people on the runway when they were told that the airport was closed. They refused to get off the plane. Now, you know, you just wonder what kind of a view of things people have who make choices like that. But it was such a peaceful thing to me to realize, in spite of the fact that I had people at the other end of the line waiting for me, that Lars and I were not at the mercy of the weather, let alone of the airport.

We're not adrift in chaos. We're held in the everlasting arms. And therefore, and this makes a difference, we can be at peace and we can accept. We can say yes, Lord, I'll take it. The faculty by which I apprehend God is the faculty of faith. And my faith enables me to say, "Yes, Lord. I don't like what You're doing. I don't understand it. You're going to have to take care of those poor people at the other end that thought I was coming to speak on this particular day. But God, You're in charge." I know the One who is in

> We're not adrift in chaos. We're held in the everlasting arms.

44

charge of the universe. He's got the whole world where? In His hands. And that's where I am.

So that to me is the key to acceptance: the fact that it is never for nothing. Faith, we might say, is the fulcrum of our moral and spiritual balance. Think of a see-saw. The fulcrum is the point where the see-saw rests. And my moral and spiritual balance depends on that stability of faith. And my faith, of course, rests on the bedrock that is Jesus Christ.

Now faith, like love, is not a feeling. We need to get that absolutely clear. Faith is not a feeling. Faith is a willed obedience action. Jesus said again and again, "Don't be afraid." "Fear not." "Let not your heart be troubled." "Believe in God. Believe also in Me." "Accept, take up the cross and follow."

He said if you want to be My disciples, there are three conditions. First, you must give up your right to yourself. Second, you must take up your cross. Third, you must follow. My understanding of giving up your right to yourself is saying no to yourself. And taking up the cross is saying yes to God. Lord, whatever it is You want to give me, I'll take it. Yes. Yes. Yes.

Do the next thing. That has gotten me through more agonies than anything else I could recommend.

There's an old legend, I'm told, inscribed in a parsonage in England somewhere on the sea coast, a Saxon legend that said, "Do the next thing." I don't know any simpler formula for peace, for relief from stress and anxiety than that very practical, very down-to-earth word of wisdom. Do the next thing. That has gotten me through more agonies than anything else I could recommend.

And when I found out that my husband was dead, I had gone out to the missionary aviation base in a place called Shell Mera, the edge of the jungle, to be with the other four wives as we waited for word about our husbands. And when the word finally came that all five of the men had been speared to death then, of course, we had decisions to make. Were we going to go back to our jungle stations or what were we going to do.

And I went back to my jungle station. I had never considered any other alternative because for one thing, I had been a missionary before I ever married Jim Elliot, before I was even engaged to Jim Elliot. So, nothing had changed as far as my missionary call was concerned. But I had to go back to a station where there was no other missionary and try to do the work that two of us had been doing between us. So it wasn't as though I was without things to keep me occupied.

I had a school of about forty boys to sort of oversee. I wasn't the teacher but I was in charge of things in a sense. I had a brand new church of about fifty baptized believers with no Scriptures in their hands and I was supposed to be the one doing the translating. I had a literacy class of about twelve girls that I was teaching to read in their own language so that eventually they could learn to read the Bible translation that I was working on at the same time. I had a ten-month-old baby for whom to care. I had a thousand details of running things on a jungle station like learning how to run a diesel generator, giving out medicines right and left, and delivering babies in between times.

I really didn't have time to sit down and have a pity party and sink into a puddle of self-pity. I did the next thing. And there was always a next thing after that. And I have found many times in my life, such as again after the death of my second husband, just the very fact that although I was living in a very civilized house, I had dishes to wash. I had floors to clean. I had laundry to do. It was my salvation.

A couple of years ago, I had the privilege and fun of taking care of four of my grandchildren while their parents were away for a trip and had taken the newborn fifth child with them. That was the only time when I've ever had the chance to do that. My grandchildren live in Southern California and I live in the Northeast. So I'm one of the lonely grandmothers as opposed to the exhausted ones. After the first day my daughter had the thoughtfulness to call that evening. And she said, "Well momma, how are you doing?" And I said, "Well they're wonderful children and they're very obedient and everything. But I don't know whether I'm going to make it through the next four days." I was tired, to say the least. I had to ask the question that my daughter really doesn't like me to ask, "How do you do it?" Because every minute of the day I'm thinking, I'm going all day long with things that need to be done every second, but my daughter has a nursing baby which takes about six more hours in the day. I kept thinking, how does she do it? How does she do it?

So, I had to ask the question. I knew she didn't want me to. But I said, "Val, how do you do it?" She laughed on the phone and she said, "Momma, I do just what you taught me years ago. I do the next thing." She told me not to think about all the things you have to do. Just do the next thing. So I took her advice and we got through the next four days triumphantly, not just somehow. But it is acceptance that enabled me to do that because I really believed that this was not an accident.

About six weeks after Jim died, I received a letter from my mother-in-law. I had been writing letters home and trying to reassure my parents and my in-laws that God was there. Everything was fine. They were not to worry about me. They were both, my in-laws and my own parents, were just dying a thousand deaths as you can imagine. And we parents, I'm sure, suffer sometimes a hundred times more than our children suffer. Although we think that the situation is worse than it is, what we can never visualize is the way the grace of God goes to work in the person who needs it.

So my mother-in-law wrote me this letter saying she was very much afraid that I was repressing my feelings, that it wasn't normal the way I was reacting and just carrying on. I was just trying to be busy and maybe I was burying myself in my work. And she told me that eventually I was going to crack. Well then, all of a sudden my peace disappeared. And I began to wonder if she was right. Is there really no such thing as the peace that passes understanding? Can God really fulfill His Word?

I kept going back again and again to the promises that God had given me. I had them right there in my journal. Day after day God was giving me promises that just enabled me to get through. Jesus Christ, the same yesterday and today and forever. Jim died yesterday. But the same Lord was with me today. And I didn't need to worry about the next fifty years, which is a temptation for anyone who's lost someone they love. You think, "Well, I guess I could make it through supper tonight but not real sure about tomorrow or next week, let alone the next fifty years."

And in the very same mail with my mother-in-law's unsettling letter, I received a poem by Amy Carmichael which came in a form letter from her mission. The poem read, "When stormy winds against us break stablish and reinforce our will; O hear us for Thine own Name's sake, hold us in strength, and hold us still. Still as the faithful mountains stand, through the long, silent years of stress; so would we wait at Thy right hand in quietness and steadfast-ness."[15] Well that sounds pretty brave and strong, doesn't it? But listen to the last stanza, "But not of us this strength, O Lord, and not of us this constancy. Our trust is Thine eternal Word, Thy presence our security."

This vital truth was laying hold of my mind and my heart, that God really did mean what He was saying that He was right there. And one of the verses that God had given me before I went to Ecuador was in Isaiah 50, verse 7, "The Lord God will help me; therefore shall I not be confounded: therefore have I set my face like a flint, and I know that I shall not be ashamed" (KJV).

I was tempted, as all of us are, to say, "Well Lord, You promised to help me, but You do have a kind of a funny way of going about it. This is not my idea of the way God is supposed to help one of His servants who is trying to be obedient and trying to be faithful." And what does God say to an argument like that? Same thing He's always saying. "Trust Me." "Trust Me." Some day, even you will see that there's sense in this. Your suffering is never for nothing.

Now my husband Jim was a fairly good carpenter. And he built a very nice house in the jungle, a very civilized house with a cement floor and wooden walls and an aluminum roof. He even built a wonderful water system by collecting the water from the aluminum roof and then piping it into the house so that we actually had a flush toilet and a shower and a sink. And he set about filling the house with very serviceable and not terribly beautiful furniture.

But while Jim was building a piece of furniture, if there was one thing he could not stand, it was for me to hang over his shoulder. And I would say well what's this thing, you know? And what are you doing with that tool? And why do you do it this way? And how in the world are you gonna fit that thing into this? And he would tell me to get lost, when it's finished, I'd see. This brings about a very simple analogy: God is saying, "Trust Me." Accept it now. See later.

How many choices have you got to go back to those alternatives? You either believe God knows what He's doing or you believe He doesn't. You either believe He's worth trusting or you say He's not. And then, where are you? You're at the mercy of chaos not cosmos. *Chaos* is the Greek word for disorder. *Cosmos* is the word for order. We either live in an ordered universe or we are trying to create our own reality.

Acceptance is a voluntary and willed act. God was giving me something to do. The next thing was, "Yes, Lord." Accept it. And that is the key to peace. Now does it make sense to an ordinary human being to say, "Accept this suffering?" Isn't it contrary to human nature? And I want to make something very clear here because I realize every word I say can be distorted and twisted and misunderstood. I want to try my best to make very plain what I mean here when I say "accept." I'm not talking about things which can be changed and/or ought to be changed.

There are some things which can be changed that ought not to be changed. For example, a dear young man that I know decided to unload his wife and two children when the second child was one week old. And he went ahead and did that against all advice to the contrary. And a couple of years later I said to him, why? And he said it wasn't working.

Now I hear this on all sides. We all hear it, don't we? We know that this is happening on all sides. There was a situation which he thought ought to be changed, and that's the thing to do. You just have to get rid of her because this is a case of incompatibility. So when I say that there are things which can be changed but ought not to be, that might be one example. There are many things which cannot be changed. And there are things which must be changed, such as abuse of persons. So I'm not, I want us to be clear that I'm not saying accept everything, just resign yourself and the worst things that happen, you don't think a thing about it. That is not my purpose in this talk.

The Apostle Paul, remember, prayed for the removal of that thorn in his flesh. And what was the answer? He prayed three times that God would remove that thorn. And the answer was, "My grace is all you need. My grace is sufficient for you" (2 Cor. 12:9 RSV). And it's very interesting, it's very significant I think, that Paul says I was given a thorn in the flesh to keep me from becoming absurdly conceited. And then he says it was a messenger of Satan.

Now that seems like a contradiction because obviously it had to be God who cares whether he becomes absurdly conceited. Satan would be delighted if we become absurdly conceited. But he said, in order to keep me from becoming absurdly conceited over a particular spiritual experience—which he has just described in that chapter, 2 Corinthians 12—he said in order to keep me from that, I was given a thorn in the flesh. So it was a messenger of Satan, he says.

So if you get all hung up, thinking now is this thing from God or is it from Satan? Is this the voice of God or the voice of Satan? Stop worrying about it. You don't really need to sort that out because here's a case where the thorn was in a sense given by God as a messenger of Satan. And there's another, at least one other, example in Scripture that I can think of the same apparent contradiction where Joseph says to his brothers that it was they who sent him into Egypt. But he says God sent me to Egypt. We know that Joseph's brothers were sinning against him and yet it was God who sent him there.

So, when the answer was no about the thorn in the flesh, and was the answer of Jesus' prayer in Gethsemane, we know that there's nothing wrong with praying that God will solve our problems and heal our diseases and pay our debts and sort out our marital difficulties. It's right and proper that we should bring such requests to God. We're not praying against His will. But when the answer is no, then we know that God has something better at stake. Far greater things are at stake. There is another level, another kingdom, an invisible kingdom which you and I cannot see now but toward which we move and to which we belong.

And a verse which, to me, sums up just the things that I've been trying to say under this heading of acceptance is another seeming contradiction which I found in the 116th Psalm. The psalmist says, "What shall I render unto the LORD, for all his benefits toward me?" (v. 12 KJV). And I was reading this one day when I was so overwhelmed with gratitude for all the blessings of my life. That I was just sitting in a chair looking out over the ocean and I was looking at this magnificent view in a very comfortable room and just saying, "Lord, I don't know how to thank You. How can I say thanks?" And I opened my Bible to this verse where the psalmist says, "What

> *When the answer is no, then we know that God has something better at stake. Far greater things are at stake. There is another level, another kingdom, an invisible kingdom which you and I cannot see now but toward which we move and to which we belong.*

shall I render?" And then I saw that the next verse is, "I will take the cup of salvation" (v. 13 KJV). What shall I give You Lord? And the answer is, I will take the cup of salvation.

Now what is in God's cup of salvation? Obviously, the psalmist in the Old Testament times was not thinking of salvation in the somewhat narrow terms that we sometimes do. Whatever is in the cup that God is offering to me, whether it be pain and sorrow and suffering and grief along with the many more joys, I'm willing to take it because I trust Him. Because I know that what God wants for me is the very best. I will receive this thing in His name.

I need pain sometimes because God has something bigger in mind. It is never for nothing. And so I say Lord, in Jesus' name, by Your grace I accept it.

Whatever is in the cup that God is offering to me, whether it be pain and sorrow and suffering and grief along with the many more joys, I'm willing to take it because I trust Him.

Chapter 4

Gratitude

First, we talked about truth, the terrible truth which is the facts of life, the twisted and fallen world that we live in. And then the wonderful facts that deal with another world, another level, another perspective. Both are true. We need to keep them in perspective.

Abraham looked at the facts of his life, his own age and his wife's barrenness, and it says he staggered not at the promise of God. He looked clearly at the facts. And Christians ought to be people who are prepared to look most steadily at the facts, the awful facts. And then look at the other level on which those facts may be interpreted and stagger not at the promise of God. So that was chapter one.

And the second chapter was on the message. God will go to any lengths to get our attention long enough to say, I am the Lord. I love you. My will for you is joy. And so if we can remember those two aspects—the truth, the message— then it will be easier for us to say yes, Lord. Acceptance.

Paul accepted the thorn even though it wasn't to his taste and preferences. Jesus accepted the cup and said not My will but Thine be done. And that same vision and that same principle ought to characterize each of us Christians as we receive, from the hand of God, the cup of salvation with whatever it contains for our ultimate redemption and perfection. There will be nothing in that cup of salvation except what is necessary.

So, having said all of that, can we then thank God? Gratitude is the subject at hand for us now. And I'd like to give you three things to think about under this subject. First of all, I'd like for us to think about two things that ought to distinguish Christians from the rest of the world. And to be quite honest, as I travel around and meet all kinds and varieties of Christians, I'm dismayed to notice that very often there doesn't seem to be any difference in the way they live and the way the rest of the world lives, in the way they respond to the experiences of their lives and the way the world would respond. In other words, if they were arrested for being Christians, would there be sufficient evidence to convict them? And I'm always asking myself the question, what kind of a difference would I expect others to see in my life which would at least catch their attention and make them say there is something different about that woman?

I said in my book, *Let Me Be a Woman*, that I'm not a different kind of a Christian because I'm a woman. But I most certainly ought to be a very different kind of a woman because I'm a Christian. Do you know people to whom you can point and say, look at him? There is a Christian. Watch that woman's life. She is a Christian. What kind of evidence would your friends see in your life?

Two things that certainly ought to distinguish you and me and everyone who calls himself a Christian are acceptance and gratitude. And it's very difficult to draw a sharp distinction between them. If we can accept a gift, then we can say thank you. Now we all have the experience of receiving all kinds of gifts from friends and relatives and great-aunts and people for which we have to say thank you, but we really aren't exactly tickled with their choice. I mean, how many crocheted toilet paper covers can a woman use? If that's Aunt Susie's thing, then you receive it every Christmas and every birthday, perhaps, from her. And the only thing that really is required of the recipient is to say thank you.

But when we're talking about the gifts of God, we're talking about gifts that come from One who knows exactly what we need even though it is not necessarily to our tastes and preferences. And He gives us everything that is appropriate to the job that He wants us to do. And so, understanding that, then we can say yes, Lord. I'll take it. It would not have been my choice but knowing You love me, I will receive it and I understand that someday I'm going to understand the necessity for this thing. So I accept it. And then I can even go the step beyond and say thank You. Thank You, Lord.

Paul says that in everything we ought to give thanks. It's not the experiences of our lives that change us. It is our response to those experiences.[16] And that should be a very noticeable distinction between the Christian and the non-Christian.

I mentioned in an earlier chapter the responses of various people that I saw in Logan Airport one day when the airport was closed. There was a great variety of responses there from tears to anger to resignation and peace. We all know people who have gone through terrible things and have turned out to be pure gold. I think every one of us knows somebody like that who has been through awful things and yet that hot fire has refined that steel or that gold. We also know people who have been through equally bad things, maybe not quite as bad, but they have turned out to be angry, bitter, resentful, querulous, and generally un-get-along-withable.

Now what was the difference? It wasn't the experiences. It was their response. And the response of a Christian should be gratitude. Thank You, Lord. I'll take this. I think we could divide the world into two classes: the people who make a habit of complaining about what they haven't got or what they have got and those who make a habit of saying "Thank You, Lord" for what they haven't got and what they have got. And you remember my basic definition of suffering: having what you don't want and wanting what you don't have, which covers the whole gamut from the smallest things like a toothache or taxes to a tumor.

It was very unsettling for me when I lived with that jungle tribe called Aucas, the so-called stone-age savages that killed my husband. I had the opportunity a couple of years after their deaths to live with those people and to get to know the people who actually did the killing. And I lived in a house with no walls. Everybody lived in a house with no walls. So this gave me an opportunity to observe very closely virtually everything that went on day and night.

And I was also under the most relentless and keen scrutiny from them because I was a freak in their midst, and everything I did was not only freakish but highly hilarious and also worth imitating. So I got a lot of that. I really had never thought of myself as a comedian until I lived with the Auca Indians and I discovered that I was expected to be non-stop entertainment.

But one of the things that stood out to me in my observations of their family life was that they never complained about anything. And my daughter, of course, grew up there in the jungle with Indians. And she was three years old when we went to live with the Aucas. She had lived with other Indians before that, and we went back later and lived with other Indians again.

But her husband made a statement to me which I'm sure my husband, maybe I should say I'm sure none of my husbands, could possibly make about me. Walt said to me about Valerie one day, he said, "You know, that woman never complains about anything." And of course, my mother's heart just swelled with pride and I suddenly realized that I probably had nothing whatsoever to do with that. In fact, it was in spite of me rather than because of me that my son-in-law could say that, because number one, Valerie is more an Elliot than she is a Howard and the Elliots were much more cheerful people. I come from a long line of pessimists on both sides. Champion pessimists.

But I realized that probably the major reason why is that she had grown up with Indians who never complained. We lived in a place where there was terrible weather. We had 144 inches of rain per year, which is twelve feet. And so when we traveled, which was always by foot and trail and sometimes canoe, we generally got soaked. We got mud sometimes splashed from head to foot, but at least up to your knees. And we were at the mercy of gnats and mud and mildew and mosquitoes and various other discomforts.

And the Indians would come from maybe a four-hour walk over the trail with say a fifty-pound basket of food on their backs—the women anyway (the men couldn't carry fifty pounds but the women could). And I never once saw a woman take that tumpline off her forehead and set her basket down and say, whew. Never. They just didn't do that.

Now these people were not Christians. And to my shame I say that I saw among them a cheerfulness, a gracious and peaceful and serene acceptance of what we would consider very hostile conditions which was taken for granted. No one was patting himself on the back because he didn't complain. So, let's take a lesson or two from those simple people and make a habit instead of complaining of saying thank You, Lord.

My daughter is dealing with probably one of the most difficult questions that parents have to deal with in training their children, and that's whining. Her children are obedient. They've learned that. They know that daddy and momma mean exactly what they say. But they don't necessarily do it cheerfully. They don't do it necessarily with a smile. And sometimes one of them has to get sent back to his bedroom until he finds a nice face. Val or Walt will say, now we really don't like that face. We don't like that tone of voice. You go back into the bedroom. And when you find a nice face or a cheerful voice, then you can come back.

And Amy Carmichael, missionary to India who's biography I wrote called *A Chance to Die,* told how when she was growing up in a little village in Northern Ireland, they not only immediately stretch forth their hand for the spanking which was given by a small paddle called a pandy, but they had to say thank you, mother. That's tough discipline, isn't it?

I had a very charming young lady staying with me once who told me this wonderful story about the kind of difference that Jesus Christ made in her own life when she was probably about eighteen years old. And this is the sort of story that I'm always looking for. And it thrills my soul to see that there is a practical, down-to-earth, visible difference that Jesus Christ has made in somebody's life.

And she said she had been going to, I think it was a Young Life meeting where the speaker talked about honoring your father and your mother. And she said most of the time it was going in one ear and out the other. And all of a sudden something clicked, and she said, "Oh, I'm supposed to honor my father and my mother. And my mother and I are like two cats a lot of times."

And she said, "I went home and I began to think about it and I thought oh, I can't do that. This thing about being a Christian is too much." But she said, "I began to pray that

God would help me to do that, whatever it meant. I really didn't know what it meant. But I knew that complaining and being grumpy and hard to get along with was certainly not fitting to someone who honors father and mother."

She went on to say, "Later, I wanted to go to a certain event and I asked my mother if I could go." She was still living at home, and so although she was seventeen or eighteen, she knew that she was under their authority. Well, her mother said she could not go to the event. And she said, "I said, okay." And then she said, "I couldn't believe my own ears. I couldn't believe it. I went into my room and I sat down and I said, whoa. It's the first time in my whole life that I haven't argued with my mother." Now that was step one in that girl's obedience to Jesus Christ.

And it's all very well to make wonderful professions about being a Christian, to do your praying and your reading and your hymn singing and go to church and do this and that and the other thing. But when it comes right down to where the rubber hits the road, what kind of a difference does it make? And that girl was able to say, "Thank You, Lord. My mother said no. It was my opportunity to obey Jesus Christ." So that's our first point for this chapter, gratitude and acceptance should distinguish the Christian.

The second thing to consider about gratitude is that it honors God. And I got this idea straight out of the Bible from the Revised Standard Version of Psalm 50, verse 23. This is what it says, "He who brings thanksgiving as his sacrifice honors me; to him who orders his way aright I will show the salvation of God!" He honors me and prepares the way so that I may show him the salvation of God.

Let me go back to October 25, 1972. That was a rather eventful day in my life. I found an apartment for my mother who was moving from Florida up to Massachusetts to be near three of her six children. So that was a major thing that happened that day. Then the son of a very close friend of mine was killed in an automobile accident. I had a visit from a young woman who had a three-year-old son with a serious heart anomaly. And we had sat down in my living room and talked about the lessons that God was teaching her through this, one of which was acceptance and gratitude. The condition was such that the doctors had told her you never know when you may find him dead in his bed or in his playpen. And there's nothing we can do until he reaches the age of four, but he may not make it to four.

It's all very well to make wonderful professions about being a Christian, to do your praying and your reading and your hymn singing and go to church and do this and that and the other thing. But when it comes right down to where the rubber hits the road, what kind of a difference does it make?

And then that very same day, my husband had to go to the hospital for a lump on his lip. And that morning I had written down on just a little piece of scratch paper these words: "How to deal with suffering of any kind." I didn't know all of the things that were going to happen in that particular day. And I don't know where this came from except I suppose from God. How to deal with suffering of any kind. Number one, I wrote, "Recognize it." Number two, "Accept it." Number three, "Offer it to God as a sacrifice." And number four, "Offer yourself with it."

Now whether I had a premonition that this thing was going to be serious or whether I was just reviewing lessons from other years, I really don't remember. But that same afternoon we were told by the doctor that my husband had cancer. The next night there was bleeding from another source which had nothing to do with that lump. We were filled with fear and resentment and worry, and it was all terribly real for both of us and necessitated our coming to Christ for a refuge.

You can imagine the dialogues that I began having with God at that point. "Lord, haven't we been through this once before? You took husband number one. Now surely, Lord, You wouldn't take Ad, would You?" And it was as if the Lord said, "I might. Trust Me." So I had to begin all over again, I thought, learning lessons that I really thought I had learned well enough before. I was saying, "Lord, did I flunk the test? Do we have to go over this again?" And the answer was, "Yes, you have to go over it again."

Now where do you turn? What do you do? You cry. You pray. You ask why? But then there's a much better thing to do that is stated in this verse that I read you. "He who brings thanksgiving as his sacrifice honors me; to him who orders his way aright I will show the salvation of God!" (Ps. 50:23 RSV). Now there are a good many circuitous routes to learning to know God. But there are some shortcuts. And I'm here to suggest that gratitude is one of those shortcuts. Just start thanking God in advance because no matter what is about to happen, you already know that God is in charge. You are not adrift in a sea of chaos.

So, what is there to be grateful for in the midst of suffering? Well, God is still love. Nothing has changed that. God is still God. He's sovereign. He's got the whole world in His hands. He knew that my husband was going to get cancer on that particular day, or that we would find out about it on that particular day. Before the foundation of the world, He knew that. So He wasn't taken by surprise. Love still wills my joy. Now I can always thank God for all of those things. Those are the facts along with these other horrible things with which we can hardly cope. It prepares the way so that I may show Him the salvation of God.

Just start thanking God in advance because no matter what is about to happen, you already know that God is in charge. You are not adrift in a sea of chaos.

So when we went to the doctor again about the second problem, we discovered he had a second kind of cancer. The two things were totally unrelated. And as we walked across the parking lot my husband began to quote from Gray's poem "Elegy Written in a Country Churchyard," "The curfew tolls the knell of parting day."[17] And I could see that he had taken already a view of total despair. His first wife had died of cancer. His father had died from the kind of cancer which he had just discovered he had.

I went back praying that God would keep me from tears, particularly since I was going to my brother's house for supper that night, and I thought, I can't be sitting there dissolved in tears. I prayed that he would take my anxieties and my fears. And that He would deliver me from making a career out of my troubles, which is a lesson that that young woman who had the little boy with the serious heart anomaly had pointed out to me just a week before. She said, "I realized that I could make a career out my child's illness. I began to pray that God would free me from that in order that I might serve others." That lesson had sunk deeply into my heart. How little I realized how desperately I was going to need that.

Love still wills my joy.

And so I thought of a little Chinese song, not that I speak Chinese but I heard that this song was sung by Chinese refugees in World War II. "I will not be afraid. I will not be afraid. I will look upward and travel onward and not be afraid."[18] Then God reminded me of Psalm 56:3 where He said, "What time I am afraid, I will trust in You" (KJV). And Psalm 34:1 that says, "I will bless the LORD at all times: his praise shall continually be in my mouth" (KJV).

Now that's a willed, conscious, deliberate obedience, isn't it? I will bless the Lord regardless of what's happening around here because there is that other level, that other perspective, a different vision. The visible things are transitory. It is the invisible things that are really permanent. The doctor's verdict was fact. I had to believe it. But God's Word was also fact.

I was able to write in my journal these words, which I certainly would have forgotten if they weren't there in black and white: "Good and peaceful all day." That was my feelings. Good and peaceful. Does that make any sense from any other standpoint except the perspective of eternity? It can't possibly make sense to anybody else. That's why it isn't explanations that we need. It's a person. We need Jesus Christ, our refuge, our fortress, the stronghold of my life. It takes desolation to teach us our need of Him.

Think of the miracles in the New Testament that Jesus performed. If you were to go through the whole New Testament and make a list of the situations that people were in when Jesus arrived, some of them were relatively trivial. For example, the embarrassed host at the wedding of Cana where the wine had run out. Now people don't really, desperately need wine

We need Jesus Christ, our refuge, our fortress, the stronghold of my life. It takes desolation to teach us our need of Him.

all the time. I guess back then it was pretty much one of the staple foods. But you don't really need seconds at a party, do you? And yet, when the wine ran out, the first miracle Jesus performed was to provide not only seconds for the party but better wine than the host had been able to serve on the first round.

If the wine hadn't run out, the people would not have been prepared to recognize Jesus in the way that they did. When there was 5,000 or 15,000 or 20,000 people who were in need of food on the mountain when Jesus had been preaching to them, the disciples said they needed food for them, but they probably could have made it home. I don't think they would have starved to death between the mountain and their own houses. It was a relatively small thing. But it was a miracle and it was in that situation.

So, what is your place of need today? Has the wine run out? Are you hungry? Is it something more desperate like the man who had been crippled for thirty-eight years or the child who had died or the widow who had lost her only son or the baby born blind or the storm that came up when the disciples thought they were perishing? What is your place of need? Where is Jesus putting His finger in your life today? Maybe there is an unanswered prayer that you have been battering away at God's door for years about, and it just seems as though He's not paying attention. Maybe there's some deep resentment in your heart because somebody has hurt you, somebody has done something which humanly speaking is unforgiveable.

Forgiveness is for real offenses. It's not like saying, "excuse me" when you step on somebody's toe by accident. "Excuse me" is one thing. But "forgive me" is for real offenses. And Jesus comes into our lives in these places of need. And if we recognize Him because of our need, then we can receive whatever it is that He is prepared to offer us whether it's the grace of forgiveness or the patience to wait for the answer to that prayer or healing or serenity in the midst of the worst times of your life. Whatever it is, you can receive it and say, "Thank You, Lord."

I have never thanked God for cancer. I have never thanked God specifically that certain Indians murdered my husband. I don't think I need to thank God for the cancer or for the murder. But I do need to thank God that in the midst of that very situation the world was still in His hands. The One who keeps all those galaxies wheeling in space is the very hand that holds me. The hands that were wounded on the cross are the same hands that hold the seven stars. The hands that were laid on old John when he was there on the Island of Patmos, and the voice that was like the sound of many waters said to him, don't be afraid. I AM. I have the keys.

At the beginning of this chapter, I referenced that I was going to tell you three things relevant to gratitude in the midst of suffering, and I don't think I've specified what that third thing is, but I've already said it. The first thing was that gratitude and acceptance distinguish the Christian. The second was that gratitude honors God. And the third principle relevant to gratitude in the face of suffering comes from the second half of the same verse I referenced earlier, Psalm 50, verse 23. "He who brings thanksgiving as his sacrifice honors me; to him who orders his way aright I will show the salvation of God!" (RSV). It prepares the way. It is in these very situations which are so painful—having what you don't want, wanting with all your heart something that you don't have—that thanksgiving can prepare the way for God to show us His Salvation.

Ten weeks after that doctor's office visit I wrote in my journal, "One down, twenty-nine to go. Ad had his first betatron treatment yesterday. Three and a half minutes under the eye of a machine the size of a freight car making the noise of three motor boats. Danger, high voltage signs in the hallway, nuclear medicine on the door, alarm system. This morning snow on the ground. The bare dogwood trees against a blue sky. The little raggedy form of McDuff [he was my Scottish terrier] running in the snow. All these things in the action of the betatron and we, ourselves, held in the hand that held the seven stars. The hand that is now laid on us again with love. And His loving words, fear not. Don't be afraid. I am the one who died. I am alive and I have the keys."

Remember Elisha and his servant sitting there on the mountain and suddenly the mountain was full of horses and chariots of fire round about Elisha. They hadn't been able to see them except with the eye of faith. Similarly, you and I have no idea of the things that are going on in the unseen world, except we do have an idea that they are for our perfection, for our fulfillment, for our ultimate blessing.

I close this chapter with one more verse from the Psalms, specifically, Psalm 55:22, "Cast your burden on the LORD and He shall sustain you" (NKJV). To my amazement and delight I discovered that that word *burden* in the Hebrew is the same word as the word for *gift*. This is a transforming truth to me. If I thank God for this very thing which is killing me, I can begin dimly and faintly to see it as a gift. I can realize that it is through that very thing which is so far from being the thing I would have chosen, that God wants to teach me His way of salvation. I will take the cup of salvation and call on the name of the Lord. I will say yes, Lord. I will say thank You, Lord.

*It is in these very situations which
are so painful—having what
you don't want, wanting with all
your heart something that you
don't have—that thanksgiving
can prepare the way for God
to show us His Salvation.*

⚘ Chapter 5 ⚘

Offering

We now turn our attention to offering. If God has given us a gift, it's never only for ourselves. It's always to be offered back to Him and very often it has repercussions for the life of the world. Jesus offered Himself to be bread for the life of the world. He said the bread that I will give is my body and I give it for the life of the world. For a Christian, the pattern is Jesus. What did He do? He offered Himself, a perfect and complete sacrifice, for the love of God. And you and I should be prepared, also, to be broken bread and poured out wine for the life of the world.

Think of the gifts of others whom you know that have been a great blessing and joy to you. I think of the gift of music. I have a nephew who is a concert violinist, who has a tremendous gift. But he doesn't just play his violin all by himself in his little apartment. That gift is for the sake of the world. And I believe that that's true of every gift that God gives to us in some way, which is not always apparent right at the beginning. Among the great gifts of my life are my husband, my daughter, and my grandchildren—and there are times when I can be very selfish about those gifts. And yet I have to recognize that they're not just for me. But these, also, that I think of as my own, must be held with an open hand and offered back to God along with my body and all that I am.

You're familiar with Paul's word from Romans 12:1, "I beseech you, therefore, brethren, by the mercies of God, that ye present your bodies a living sacrifice, holy, acceptable unto God, which is your reasonable service" (KJV). I particularly like the KJV translation as it translates that last phrase as "an act of intelligent worship." Now if I present to God my body as a living sacrifice then that includes everything that the body contains—my brains, my personality, my heart, my emotions, my will, my temperament, my prejudices, my failings, all the rest of it—is presented to God as a living sacrifice. God has, after all, given me a body to live in. Everything in my life I begin to see as a gift and I do mean everything.

Now that may seem like sheer poppycock to some of you. But I hope that in the context of the things that I've been saying you'll begin to see that everything can be seen as a gift, even my widowhood. I began very slowly to recognize, after my first husband was killed, that it was within the context of widowhood that God wanted me to glorify Him. It was not my idea. It was something that God not only allowed, but in a very real sense, which I began slowly to understand, He had given me because He had something else in mind. And this was a gift not just for me, but also for the life of the world in some mysterious sense that I did not need to understand because I could trust Him.

Under this idea of considering how an offering relates to the idea of suffering, I want to consider three things and then I'll expound on those. First, everything is a gift. Second, there are several kinds of offerings that I can make to God. Or, we could say that we want to think about an offering as a sacrifice, and when I use the word sacrifice with regard to my own life, the emphasis is not on loss and desolation and giving up. The emphasis is on the fact that God has given me something that I can offer back to Him. We'll come to that a little bit later. And third, the greatest, is the offering of obedience.

When I get up in the morning I do try to make it a practice to do some of my praying first thing in the morning. It's a good thing to talk to God before you start talking to anybody else. I try to begin my prayers with thanksgiving. There's always a long list of things for which to be thankful. One of them is I can get up in the morning, that I can be in a comfortable place, looking out over a very beautiful view. I thank God for the sleep of a night, for health and strength and for work to do.

I'm very grateful for work. I think about somebody like Joni Eareckson Tada and what Joni wouldn't give to just have a chance to wash dishes maybe one time or do the worst job that you and I might hate. Thank God that you can get up. I thank Him for my house and my husband and my health and the money that we have and the food that we have and clothes for our backs and grandchildren and my daughter and on and on and on. And you all have equally long lists, I'm sure.

But then I don't always find it easy to include on that list the thorn in the flesh, the word that my husband spoke to me which hurt me—as he does that once in a while. I'm married to a sinner. I don't know what you other married women are married to. But as far as I know, there really isn't anything else to marry. And it's always a good exercise for me to remember that my poor husband is also married to a sinner. So I thank God for that husband with his imperfections, which are not very many. But I thank Him for the particular set of gifts that He has given me in that man which I can offer back to God with thanksgiving.

When Joseph was taken into captivity he could not possibly have imagined what God had in mind years later. But in Genesis 45:8 we read Joseph's words to his brothers: "It was not you who sent me here, but God" (NIV). What looked like a horrible thing, jealous brothers hating their younger brother, wanting to get rid of him, deciding to kill him, then realizing they could make some money out of him, selling him into captivity. He goes down to Egypt and is made a slave. And eventually ends up in prison and one thing and another. Does that look like a gift from God? And yet he tells his brothers that it wasn't they who sent him. It was God.

Paul spoke of being given a thorn in the flesh. Jesus referred to the cup which His Father had given Him. Now each of these things represent great suffering, not trivial things at all. Yet, Joseph was able to say, when he named his son Ephraim, "God hath caused me to be fruitful in the land of my affliction" (Gen. 41:52 KJV). It's not the experience that changed him. It was his response. Joseph trusted God. Now what is God's intention when He gives you and me something? He is giving me something in my hands with which I can turn to Him and offer it back to Him with thanksgiving.

I remember when I was a little girl wanting to buy Christmas presents for my parents and I had no way at all of earning money. My brothers had paper routes and earned maybe twenty-five cents a week or something like that back in the Depression days. But I had to depend on an allowance. So I would have had absolutely nothing to give to my mother for Christmas if my mother hadn't given something to me first. That's the way it is with us with God, isn't it? We are totally destitute. Everything that we have comes from Him and we have nothing to offer except what He has given us.

There's an old prayer of thanksgiving at the offering time. It goes like this, "All things come of thee, O Lord and of thine own have we given thee." We receive it from Him. We accept it in our hands. We say thank You. And then we offer it back. This is the logical sequence of the things which I have been talking about. Everything is a gift. Everything is meant to be offered back.

This lesson became a powerful, life-changing, transforming lesson during the time of my husband's illness. I would awaken in those wee small hours of the night—which Amy Carmichael calls the hours when all life's molehills become mountains—my mind would be filled with vivid imaginings of the horrible things that were going to happen to my husband between then and death.

Death truly was the unarguable conclusion of what my husband had, medically speaking. There was no possibility that he was going to survive. So I had faced that fairly squarely. But the doctors were predicting hideous mutilations that they were going to practice on him between then and death, and I felt I could not stand it. In those wee small hours I began to cry out to the Lord. Then it came to me with great clarity one night, I suppose about two or three o'clock in the morning, that my agony, my vicarious anguish for my husband was something which God had put in my hands to offer back to Him. It was a gift.

Now let's think about this second component of offering relative to suffering, the idea of sacrifice. There are many occasions in Scripture where the word sacrifice is used. And it was a very important part of the Hebrew life back in Old Testament days. Blood sacrifice was a daily occurrence in the Tabernacle. And the rituals of sacrifice controlled the people's whole lives.

The Old Testament also speaks of the sacrifice of thanksgiving in Psalms. The verse that came to me in those hours of fear was a broken and a contrite heart, I will not despise. The sacrifices of God are a broken spirit, a broken and a contrite heart, I will not despise. I'm sure some of you have a broken spirit, a broken heart. God will not despise that offering if that's all you have to offer (Ps. 51:17 KJV, author paraphrase).

I have felt as if I was destitute like the widow of Zarepath. You remember the story of how Elijah was fed by ravens for a time and then God told him that the ravens were going to stop. And that he was to go down to a place called Zarepath where there was a widow who would feed him. Now I don't think we can begin to imagine the absolute dereliction of a widow in those ancient times. But she was the most helpless and poor of all.[19]

I'm sure some of you have a broken spirit, a broken heart. God will not despise that offering if that's all you have to offer (Ps. 51:17 KJV, author paraphrase).

Now why in the world would God Almighty, who owns the cattle on a thousand hills, choose a destitute woman to feed his prophet Elijah? And you remember that when Elijah reaches Zarepath he finds this woman out gathering a couple of sticks, and he asks her for a drink of water. And then he asks her for the most unreasonable request imaginable, and he says bake me a cake.

Well, if she were speaking modern English, she would have said, "Surely you've got to be kidding. I'm out here gathering two sticks so that I can bake the last handful of flour and last few drops of oil into a little cake, which is the only thing that stands between me and my son and death. We are starving to death and you ask me to bake you a cake."

But the woman recognized that this was a man of God. So to her, it was a matter of obedience to God to fulfill his request, so she baked him a cake. She believed his word that the flask of oil would not fail, nor would the barrel of meal be empty. What had God done in sending the prophet to a destitute woman? He had put into that woman's hands something to offer back. But what a pitiful offering. One little handful of flour, a few drops of oil.

Do you remember when the little boy brought his lunch to Jesus (or the disciples extorted that lunch from him). He had five loaves and two fishes which the disciples brought to Jesus and he put it into Jesus' hands. One of the disciples even asked Jesus what good that little bit of food could be for such a large crowd.

Now I'm speaking to some of you who feel as if you have nothing whatsoever to offer to God. You don't have any huge sufferings, perhaps. You don't have any great gifts. You were behind the door when they gave out the gifts and you feel like, poor me, I can't sing and I can't preach and I can't pray and I can't write books and I can't be the hostess with the mostest. So I really can't serve the Lord. If I had *that person's* gifts *then* it would be a different story.

I don't know who I'm talking to but I'm sure that there are some of you who would be saying, what is the good of my offering for such a crowd. You're telling me that I have something that is going to matter for the life of the world? And I say, yes, that's what I'm telling you. Because God takes a widow with nothing, God takes a little boy's lunch and He turns that into something for the good of the world because that individual let it go.

I began to see, again very dimly. Please don't imagine that I was some kind of spiritual giant to see this thing. It was the Holy Spirit of God that said to me, give it to Me. Let it go. Offer it up. A sacrifice. Something in your hands to give Me. How does a mother feel when her tiny little two-year-old comes into the house with a smashed dandelion clenched in his little, sweaty fist and he offers her the smashed dandelion? It means everything in the world because love transforms it. That's what this is about. Suffering and love are inextricably bound up together. And love invariably means sacrifice.

We talked about the sacrifice of fathers and mothers. What about the sacrifice of husbands and wives? What about the sacrifice of those who are prepared to be single for the rest of their lives for the glory of God? I think of Amy Carmichael. She believed that God was actually calling her to remain single and it scared her.

Suffering and love are inextricably bound up together. And love invariably means sacrifice.

She felt that she might, perhaps, be desolate with loneliness. And God brought to her mind the words from Psalm 34:22, "None of them that trust in him shall be desolate" (KJV). And out of that offering, that brokenness, that living sacrifice which was the life of Amy Carmichael, came a great missionary work that continued for decades.

Amy Carmichael, a single woman, became the mother of thousands of Indian children. There was a time when the family that she founded as a Dohnavur Fellowship—little children, rescued from temple prostitution—that family numbered over 900 people at one time. And she worked there for fifty-three years. And she wrote these words in one of her poems, "If Thy dear home be fuller, Lord, for that a little emptier my house on earth, what rich reward that guerdon[20] were." You and I have no idea what God has in mind when we make the offering. But everything is potential material for sacrifice.

Again and again, I've had people say to me, how do you handle loneliness? And I say that I can't handle loneliness. They ask, "Well didn't you spend a lot of time alone in the jungle?" I inevitably reply, "Yes, I did. I spent a good many more years alone than I did married." They return, "Well how did you handle it?" To which I reply, "I didn't. I couldn't. I have to turn it over to Somebody who can handle it." In other words, my loneliness became my offering.

And so if God doesn't always remove the feeling of loneliness, it is in order that every minute of every day, perhaps, I have something to offer up to Him and say, "Lord, here it is. I can't handle this." I don't know what your emotions may be that you can't handle, but I believe that every one of us knows something about loneliness. Singles always imagine that married people are not lonely, but I can testify that there are different kinds of loneliness.

I have never forgotten what a missionary speaker said in chapel when I was a student. We had compulsory chapel five days a week at Wheaton College. So we heard hundreds of speakers and remembered practically nothing of most of them. But I have never forgotten what this woman said. She spoke about the little boy bringing his lunch to Jesus. And she said, "If my life is broken when given to Jesus, it may be because pieces will feed a multitude when a loaf would satisfy only a little boy."

What have you got in your hand to give to Him? Is it a gift that you recognize as a gift, a talent for example? Is it the willingness to be a mother and to take the criticism of the women who say that a woman who's got half a brain will put her children in somebody else's care and get out and do something "fulfilling"? Is it the willingness to take the flack from the rest of the world about something that you've decided to do for Jesus' sake? Is it the willingness to be unrecognized, unappreciated?

You know, we've got a very twisted idea of this word *ministry*. We think that a ministry means just a very short list of things: preaching or singing or doing a seminar or writing a book or teaching a Sunday school class. Of course those are ministry. They're forms of service. But the word ministry just means *service*. And service is a part of our offering to God.

People would think of my ministry as being my missionary work, my writing, my speaking. But you know, I don't spend most of my life standing at a podium. I spend most of my life sitting at a desk, standing at a sink, standing at an ironing board, going to the grocery store, sitting in airports, doing a whole lot of things which are not anything for which I expect to get medals. They are moments to be offered to Jesus. Do the next thing.

Which brings me to my third component of offering relative to suffering, the offering of obedience. When my brother, Tom, was a little boy about three years old, one of his favorite forms of play was to take all the paper bags out of the drawer in the kitchen where my mother kept them and spread them all over the floor. Well, my mother permitted that with Tom. He was number five. I was number two. And I don't think I would have gotten away with it. But she'd learned a lot of things by that time and I'm sure she was tired.

She told him that he could do that on one condition, that he put the bags back in the drawer before he left the kitchen. Well, he understood that perfectly well. Children usually understand far more than we think they do. So she came into the kitchen one day and there were the paper bags all over the floor but no sign of Tom. So she found him in the living room where my father was playing the piano, playing hymns. And my mother said, "Tommy, I want you to come put the bags back in the drawer." And he looked up with a smile of the most innocent and seraphic sweetness and he said, "But I wanna sing 'Jesus Loves Me.'" And my father stopped playing the piano and took the opportunity to press home a profound lesson: to obey is better than sacrifice.

It's no good singing "Jesus Loves Me" when you're disobeying your mother, and the highest form of worship is obedience. What do I have to offer to God that is more important than my obedience? There's a great lesson on this in the book of Ezekiel, hidden back in the 24th chapter, beginning in verse 16. God told the son of man, "I take away from you the desire of your eyes with one stroke; yet you shall neither mourn nor weep, nor shall your tears run down. Sigh in silence, make no mourning for the dead; bind your turban on your head, and put your sandals on your feet; do not cover your lips, and do not eat man's bread of sorrow" (Ezek. 24:16–17 NKJV). In other words, forget all the ritual signs of mourning. And Ezekiel replies this, "So I spoke to the people in the morning, and at evening my wife died; and the next morning I did as I was commanded" (Ezek. 24:18 NKJV). Now that's a very short description of some pretty important things! In the evening my wife died, and the next morning I did as I was commanded.

I have discovered that there is no consolation like obedience. And when I was trying to offer up my feelings to God in those wee small hours of the morning, I thanked God when it was time to get up because there were all kinds of just simple, ordinary, down-to-earth things to do. Do the next thing.

God gave to the widow of Zarepath and to the little boy and to Ezekiel something to give back to Him, something that would matter very much to others. God enabled Ezekiel to give his sorrow back to Him and to get up and do what he was commanded to do for the life of the world. It wasn't just Ezekiel that God was interested in there. God wanted to make Ezekiel into broken bread and poured out wine for the life of the world.

Let me ask you, who are the people who have most profoundly influenced your life? Those who have most profoundly influenced my life are without exception people who have suffered because it has been in that very suffering that God has refined the gold, tempered the steel, molded the pot, broken the bread and made that person into something that feeds a multitude—of whom I have been one of the beneficiaries.

I once received a wonderful letter from a woman, an older woman who told me back when she was a little girl in the Depression that her father had died. None of his friends came to the funeral. She had to wear a borrowed dress. The house was mortgaged. Her mother was left a widow with seven children. And the lawyer who was supposed to be handling her financial affairs stole the inheritance. And the lady said this, when we went back to the house after the funeral, my mother picked up a broom and began to sweep the kitchen. And she said I look back on that now and I realize that it was the soft swish, swish, swish of that broom that began the healing process. She said my mother was a destitute woman. And when people asked her years later how she made it, she just said, "I prayed." Well she didn't just pray. She prayed and she did the next thing. She picked up the broom.

And so I say to you today, God has put something in your hand that you can accept. You can say, thank You, Lord. And then you can offer it back to Him. Let me give you another verse that encourages me tremendously. Psalm 119 verse 91 says, "They continue this day according to Your ordinances, for all are Your servants" (NKJV).

What's happening in your life today? Is it good? Then it's easy to thank God for, isn't it? Is it bad? If you can remember that this day, like every other day, His ordinances stand fast. Those eternal realities are unshakable. His Word is infrangible. The world and all its passionate desires will one day disappear. The man who is following the will of God is part of the permanent and cannot die. I encourage you to make an offering of your sufferings.

Ugo Bassi said this, "Measure your life by loss and not by gain, not by the wine drunk, but by the wine poured forth. For love's strength standeth in love's sacrifice, and he that suffereth most hath most to give."[21]

*I have discovered that there is
no consolation like obedience.*

Chapter 6

Transfiguration

Back in 1820 there was a little six-week-old baby who had an inflammation of the eyes. And the doctor applied hot poultices and burned the corneas so that the child was blind for life. When she was nine years old she wrote these words, "O what a happy soul am I although I cannot see. I'm resolved that in this world contented I shall be. So many blessings I enjoy that other people don't. To weep and sigh because I'm blind, I cannot nor I won't."[22]

And that little girl grew up to write 8,000 hymns— among them, "To God Be the Glory," "Blessed Assurance," "Rescue the Perishing," "Face to Face." Her name was Fanny Crosby. I had heard the story of Fanny Crosby years ago but I hadn't come across that little poem until much later, written at the age of nine. "To weep and sigh because I'm blind, I cannot nor I won't." I love that.

And there's a verse in the 58th chapter of Isaiah, which very nicely links together what I said about offering in the last chapter with what I want to address with you now.

Transfiguration. These are the words from Isaiah 58:10–11, "If you pour yourself out for the hungry and satisfy the desire of the afflicted, then shall your light rise in the darkness and your gloom be as the noonday. And the LORD will guide you continually, and satisfy your desire with good things, and make your bones strong; and you shall be like a watered garden, like a spring of water, whose waters fail not" (RSV).

It's that deep principle articulated here that I want to talk to you about. I've given it the one-word title of *transfiguration*. I've chosen that word rather than *transformation*. The two are almost identical. But I love the word transfiguration because it implies an aspect of glory that is not always implied in the word transformation.

Transfiguration. You remember the story of Jesus on the Mount when He was transfigured. The two things—suffering and glory—are brought into contact because it was about suffering that Moses and Elijah were speaking when Jesus was transfigured. And this verse from Isaiah speaks of pouring yourself out for the hungry and receiving, in exchange, the satisfaction of your own needs, strength of limb. You will be like a well-watered garden, like a spring whose waters never fail.

I think Fanny Crosby, at the tender age of nine, had begun to glimpse the fact that there was more joy in giving than there would ever be in receiving. And she was broken bread and poured out wine for the life of the world. Only God knows the ripple effect of Fanny Crosby's obedience in the offering up of herself. In Proverbs 11:25 we read,

"The generous man will be prosperous, and he who waters will himself be watered" (NASB). I'm sure that all of us who have ever tried that therapy have found it to be extremely effective.

The idea of transfiguration follows very naturally and logically from acceptance, gratitude, and offering. If we receive the things that God wants to give us, if we thank Him for them and if we make those things an offering back to God, then this is what's going to happen—transfiguration, the great principle of exchange that is the central principle of the Christian faith—the cross. We know that the cross does not exempt us from suffering. In fact, the cross is a symbol of suffering. In fact, Jesus said you must take up your cross.

There are kinds of suffering which we would never have to endure if we were not believers. We read that through much tribulation we must enter into Heaven. And Jesus explained that if we are His followers, then they are going to arrest us, imprison us, drag us into court, and even the day will come when they will kill us and think that they're doing God a favor. He told us these things so that when they do happen, our faith in Him will not be shaken. If your faith rests in your idea of how God is supposed to answer your prayers, your idea of heaven here on earth or pie in the sky or whatever, then that kind of faith is very shaky and is bound to be demolished when the storms of life hit it. But if your faith rests on the character of Him who is the eternal I AM, then that kind of faith is rugged and will endure.

I'm very keenly, painfully aware of the fact that this message on suffering is barely skimming the surface. And I think of the words of one of the ancient mystics who said that God is a mountain of corn from which I, like a sparrow, pluck a single kernel. That describes what I've succeeded in doing if I have succeeded in doing anything at all. Perhaps we've plucked a single kernel, just enough to satisfy the hunger of a tiny bird from this immense mountain of corn, which is the reality of God Himself.

We've thought about the truth, the terrible truth, the message, the matter of acceptance, of gratitude and of offering. Now let us think about transfiguration. Again, I'll give you three principles that connect transfiguration to suffering. This time I will help by adding alliteration. I don't work very hard trying to get things alliterative, but it happens to be three Ps this time: the principle of, the perspective, and the paradoxes.

The first principle is that of the cross: Life comes out of death. I bring God my sorrows and He gives me His joy. I bring Him my losses and He gives me His gains. I bring Him my sins, He gives me His righteousness. I bring Him my deaths and He gives me His life. But the only reason God can give me His life is because He gave me His death.

So these things continually work not only in the spiritual life, but in the natural world as well. Jesus used the very simple illustration of the natural world in the incident where just after His entering into Jerusalem where He was hailed with palm branches and hosannas, two of the disciples came to Him and told Him that there were some Greeks there who wanted to see Him because they had heard about the raising of Lazarus from the dead.

Well, we all love miracles and we all love a miracle worker. If you want to be popular, you perform as many miracles as possible in as visible a medium as possible and people will flock to you. People flocked to Jesus, he said, not because of the words that He spoke, but because of the loaves and fishes. In this case it was raising Lazarus from the dead about which word had spread abroad. So people were crowding into Jerusalem to see this man and the disciples came and told Jesus that they wanted to see Him.

Well, Jesus took that opportunity to turn His disciples' idea into glory upside-down. The world has an idea of what's important, what really is the glory of God. Do all the miracles that you can and get everything all sorted out and healed and paid for and solved and that's God's glory. And of course, I believe in a God who can make the sun stand still. And He can turn water into wine and make dry land out of rivers. Don't misunderstand me.

But when I hear a preacher say what you need is a miracle, I want to say, "I might think that's what I need, but very often my prayers are really asking for stones. And what God wants to give me is bread, something that will not only feed myself but feed the world as well." So I can pray. I might even pray for a miracle. I don't think I've done that very often. But when I was praying for healing for my husband's cancer, I knew that I was praying for a miracle, humanly speaking. But the bottom line was, "Lord, Thy will be done."

We need our definitions revised just as the disciples needed to have their definition of glory revised and turned upside-down. Jesus said, I'm going to show you what glory is. He said, "Now the hour has come for the Son of Man to be glorified. Verily, verily, I say unto you, except a corn of wheat fall into the ground and die, it abideth alone: but if it die, it bringeth forth much fruit" (KJV). Now that is the principle of the cross. He was on His way to the cross. Is there anything less significant and distinctive than a seed? You've seen one corn of wheat, you've seen them all. You've seen one grain, one seed, one apple seed, you've seen them all. So there isn't anything terribly distinctive, noticeable about a seed.

And when that seed falls into the ground, it's gone. It may never been seen again. But we know for sure that nothing is ever going to come out of that seed unless it falls into the ground, into the dark, into the unknown, into ignominy and death. But out of that seed, then, comes the great harvest, the golden grain. So that is the principle of exchange. I give Him my deaths and He gives me His life. My sorrows, He gives me joy. My losses, He gives me His gains. This is the great principle of the cross.

> *I give Him my deaths and He gives me His life. My sorrows, He gives me joy. My losses, He gives me His gains. This is the great principle of the cross.*

Some of you, I'm sure, know the story of George Mathison, the hymn writer, who became engaged. And while they were engaged he went blind and his fiancé, not wanting to be saddled with a blind man, broke the engagement. And it was then that George Mathison wrote those wonderful words, "O love that will not let me go. I rest my weary soul in Thee. I give Thee back"—here we are with this offering—"I give Thee back the life I owe, that in Thine ocean depths its flow may richer fuller be."[23]

And I think of the words that my first husband, Jim Elliot, wrote when he was twenty-two years old. "He is no fool who gives what he cannot keep to gain what he cannot lose." He was paraphrasing the words of Jesus, "If you lose your life for My sake, you'll find it" (Matt. 10:39, author paraphrase). He exchanges my weakness, my losses, my sins, my sorrows, my sufferings. When we offer them to Him, He has something to give us in exchange, and that might feed a multitude.

So the principle of exchange is the principle of the cross. And that principle goes all the way back to before the foundation of the world. The Lamb was slain. The blood sacrifice was made in the mind of God before there was such a thing as sin. Sacrifice and suffering and glory. There is no getting away from them.

We live in New England where we love September and October. Lars always groans about it because he's a Southerner and he thinks the winters are so long. But when the acorns begin to fall, I love the season because, for one thing, we do have the most spectacular colors in the country because we have those rock maples that turn blood red and salmon and mauve and unbelievable colors. But the glory of the autumn is a symbol of death. That blood red reminds me of blood, which is the symbol of death.

If it weren't for the oak tree letting go of all those precious little seeds, those acorns, they would never fall into the ground and die so that there would never be any more oak trees and the squirrels would starve to death. Everything that you and I eat means that something has died in some way. Even an egg, even a glass of milk, the chicken and the cow have not died, but they have given life, haven't they? And practically everything else on the table tells us that something has died, whether it's corns of wheat or animals. So life comes out of death. It is the principle of the universe, the principle of exchange. Even stars die. We're being told more and more, these fascinating things that astronomers are discovering.

But there's a verse hidden in 2 Chronicles 29, verse 27 that has been a great encouragement and cheer to me ever since I found that verse back when I was a senior in college and dying a thousand deaths over the fact that I was in love with somebody that I didn't think was ever going to be in love with me, and thinking that I was very foolish to even entertain any hopes for this man. So I put my feelings on God's altar. I can't handle a lot of my emotions. And so I just say, "Lord, here it is. You take it and You make something out of it if You can. If You can make something out of a little boy's lunch and out of the widow's cruse of oil, then maybe You can do something with this."

So I turned over all those passions, that veritable tornado of passion that I felt for this young man whose name just happened to be Jim Elliot, to God. And God gave me this verse in 2 Chronicles, "When the burnt offering began, the song of the LORD also began" (2 Chron. 29:27 NASB). Isn't that terrific? It works. When the burnt offering began, the song of the Lord began also. It's just referring to the actual ritual of sacrifice. And yet, it has implications for our spiritual lives, doesn't it?

Now, let's look at this perspective, the second principle of transfiguration tied to suffering. Our perspectives need to be transfigured, changed into something that has glory in it. And that wonderful chapter of Hebrews 11 tells me many things about perspective. It says in verse 13, after going through the stories of Abel and Enoch and Noah and Abraham and Sarah, all these impossible things that they did by faith, it says, "All these died in faith, without receiving the promises, but having seen them and having welcomed them from a distance, and having confessed that they were strangers and exiles on the earth" (NASB). Those who use such language show plainly that they are looking for a country of their own. If their hearts had been in the country they had left, they could have found opportunity to return. Instead we find them longing for a better country. And is there anything that makes you long for that better country more keenly than suffering of one sort or another?

Even as my poor little granddaughter was suffering over the fact that she'd gotten spanked three times in one day, and she said, "Oh, if only Adam and Eve hadn't sinned." Just when the washing machine runs over with company in the house, I mean you do kind of, at that point, long for a better country, don't you?

Then we see in verse 27 in the same chapter of Hebrews, speaking of Moses, "By faith he left Egypt, not fearing the wrath of the king; for he endured, as seeing Him who is unseen" (NASB). That's a transfigured perspective. Then if we go back up to verse 20 in Hebrews 11, we see that, "By faith Isaac blessed Jacob and Esau, even regarding things to come" (NASB). A transfigured perspective.

Now it's one thing to get that perspective on other people's lives, isn't it? Do you find it easier to see the will of God at work in somebody else's life than in your own? Would you like to have the story of Daniel without the lions' den? Of course we wouldn't, because we know the end of the story. Well, we Christians, we've got this whole book full of wonderful stories like that and the end of every single one of them is the same. It's glory every time.

Would you like to have the story of Joseph without all his trials and tribulations, without his going into the pit? What would you know about Shadrach, Meshach, and Abednego if they'd never gone into a fiery furnace? The blessing of Fanny Crosby's life has been enormously increased through knowing that these words of these beautiful gospel hymns came from a woman who never saw the light of day, or at least never remembered seeing it from the age of six weeks. Everything has been transfigured in their lives because we know the end of the story.

I remember when Jeannette Clift George was playing the part of Corrie Ten Boom in the movie called *The Hiding*

Place. She was interviewed on one of Billy Graham's programs. He asked her what was the characteristic, as she studied Corrie Ten Boom's life, that most impressed her about Ten Boom? And without any hesitation Jeannette's answer was, "Joy." And for all who saw Corrie Ten Boom either in person or on the screen saw a radiant old face filled with the joy of the Lord.

Now where did that come from? Was it because everything in her life worked so beautifully? Was it because she had had a happy life as the world would define happiness? Of course not. Her perspective was transfigured. And she, herself, was transfigured for the benefit of the rest of us. We were given a visible sign in the face of Corrie Ten Boom of an invisible reality—another country, another level, another perspective.

Paul was able to sing in prison. And he wrote those prison epistles which are filled with joy. The book of Philippians is called the epistle of joy. And he wrote these stunning words in the first chapter of Philippians, verse 29, words which to me are loaded. He said, "For he has graciously granted you the privilege not only of believing in Christ, but of suffering for him as well" (NRSV). You have been given a gift of suffering.

And then in Colossians, also the first chapter, verse 24, this even more stunning and loaded verse, "I am now rejoicing in my sufferings for your sake" (NRSV). Sounds like gobbledygook, doesn't it? Until he goes on to say, "I am completing what is lacking in Christ's afflictions for the sake of his body, that is, the church." Now to me that is the most profound statement about the subject that we have been discussing in all of Scripture, of human suffering. We cannot come close to the statements about the sufferings of Christ.

But Paul is in prison and he says, it is my happiness to suffer for you because this is my way of helping to complete in my poor human flesh. I understand Paul was chained between two soldiers. Can you imagine the discomfort of that, not to mention the lack of privacy, twenty-four hours a day? But in his poor human flesh, in some very mysterious way that I can never explain to you, but I believe it, he said I am helping to complete the full tale of Christ's afflictions still to be endured for what? For the sake of His body, the church.

And I know that some of you are sitting there saying but what has that got to do with my sufferings? My sufferings are not for the sake of the gospel. And for years I died a thousand deaths over that one because I thought, I've never really had any sufferings that were directly for the sake of the gospel. And even the death of my husband Jim who had attempted to take the gospel to some people, he did not get literally killed because of the word of his testimony. He had never spoken a word to those Indians. They didn't have any idea why he was there and surmised that he was a cannibal. And so they thought they'd better bump him off in self-defense before they got eaten themselves.

So for years and years I pondered this. And I have come to the conclusion that there is a mystery here much deeper than the fact that Paul was literally suffering in prison because of his testimony. Christ suffers in me. Now if I suffer because I am a member of His body, I may be a sore member, but He suffers with me and for me and in me. And when I suffer, He suffers. Christ suffered on the cross. He bore all my sins, all my griefs and all my sorrows. And yet there is a full tale yet to be fulfilled. I don't understand it. I simply affirm it. I accept it.

Finally, let's look at the paradoxes as they relate to transfiguration and suffering. We need a transfigured view of these paradoxes. Scriptural metaphors for suffering speak of pruning. The best fruit comes out of the most drastic pruning. The purest gold comes out of the hottest fires. I have certainly learned the deepest lessons of my life through going through the deepest waters. And the greatest joys come out of the greatest sorrows. Life comes out of death.

> *He bore all my sins, all my griefs and all my sorrows. And yet there is a full tale yet to be fulfilled. I don't understand it. I simply affirm it. I accept it.*

Let's think of Mary. Probably just a teenage girl who, in her humility and her poverty, offered herself, her plans, her hopes, her fears of what might be thought of her if it appeared that she had been unfaithful to her fiancé, Joseph. Her instant response to the word of God was, "Behold, the handmaid of the Lord; let it be unto me according to thy word" (Luke 1:38 kjv). And it was out of this sacrifice, this offering of herself that the Savior of the World was born. Transfiguration. She was called the most exalted among women, most highly exalted. That came from humility. If you lose your life for His sake, you'll find it.

There is, in fact, no redemptive work done anywhere without suffering. And God calls us to stand alongside Him, to offer our sufferings to Him for His transfiguration and to fill up in our poor human flesh. If I'm not given the privilege of being crucified, if I'm not given the privilege of being martyred in some way, some literal way for God, I am given the privilege of offering up to Him whatever He has given to me. I offer to Him all that I am, all that I have, all that I do and all that I suffer for His transformation, transfiguration, exchange for the life of the world. That is what it's all about.

You may be suffering as a father because your son has rejected you. You may be suffering as a son because your father rejected you thirty years ago. We have a young man living in our house right now, a student, who was rejected at the age of ten months by his father and his mother. Put into a foster home where he stayed for fifteen years.

I made a list of these amazing paradoxes. These are some of the things that the Scripture tells me God transforms. The wilderness into pasture. Deserts into springs. Perishable into imperishable. Weakness into power. Humiliation into glory. Poverty into riches. Mortality into immortality. This vile body into a resplendent body. My mourning into the oil of joy. My spirit of heaviness, He gives me in exchange a garment of praise. And beauty for ashes.

In Revelation 7:16 and 17 we read, "They shall neither hunger anymore nor thirst anymore; the sun shall not strike them, nor any heat; for the Lamb who is in the midst of the throne will shepherd them and lead them to living fountains of waters. And God will wipe away every tear from their eyes" (NKJV).

In closing, I want to give you a poem written by Grant Colfax Tuller. "My life is but a weaving between my Lord and me; I do not choose the colors, He worketh steadily. Oft times He weaveth sorrow and I, in foolish pride, forget He sees the upper, and I the under side. Not till the loom is silent and the shuttles cease to fly, shall God unroll the canvas and explain the reason why. The dark threads are as needful in the Weaver's skillful hand, as the threads of gold and silver in the pattern He has planned."[24]

Everything that happens fits into a pattern for good. Suffering is never for nothing.

There is, in fact, no redemptive
work done anywhere
without suffering.

Notes

1. C. S. Lewis, *The Problem of Pain* (New York: HarperCollins, 1940, 1996).

2. Fyodor Dostoevsky, Trans. Richard Pevear and Larissa Volokhonsky, *The Brothers Karamazov* (New York: Alfred A. Knopf, 1992 [1879]), 242 and 245.

3. F. W. H. Myers, "St. Paul," http://www.sermonindex.net/modules/newbb/viewtopic.php?topic_id=2386&forum=35.

4. Malcolm Muggeridge's book *Jesus Rediscovered* (1969). This quote can also be found in Elisabeth Elliot's book *A Path Through Suffering*.

5. Quote also quoted elsewhere by Elisabeth Elliot, original source unknown.

6. Lewis, *The Problem of Pain*, 83.

7. Ibid., 61.

8. Ibid., 23.

9. https://www.gutenberg.org/files/42557/42557-h/42557-h.htm.

10. Fanny Crosby and William Howard Doane, https://www.hymnal.net/en/hymn/h/1059.

11. "Jesus Keep Me Near the Cross" was written by Lucy Ann Bennett and James William Elliott, https://www.hymnal.net/en/hymn/h/1076.

12. Original word was *strategem*, which means a scheme and has been changed here for clarity of use.

13. George Herbert, poem entitled "Sin (I)," https://www.poetryfoundation.org/poems/44373/sin-i.

14. George MacDonald, "A Book of Strife in the Form of a Diary of an Old Soul—September," https://www.poeticous.com/george-macdonald/a-book-of-strife-in-the-form-of-the-diary-of-an-old-soul-september.

15. Poem titled "Security," in *Mountain Breezes: The Collected Poems of Amy Carmichael*.

16. Ephesians 5:20.

17. Thomas Gray, "Elegy Written in a Country Churchyard," https://www.poetryfoundation.org/poems/44299/elegy-written-in-a-country-churchyard.

18. Written by Annie Flint Johnson, https://www.hymnal.net/en/hymn/h/678.

19. See 1 Kings 17.

20. *Guerdon* is a reward or something by which amends is made. Amy Carmichael, "Let Me Not Shrink," in *Mountain Breezes: The Collected Poems of Amy Carmichael*.

21. Sermon by Ugo Bassi, source unknown.

22. Fanny J. Crosby, *Memories of Eighty Years* (Boston: J. H. Earle & Co., 1906), 25–26, https://archive.org/details/memoriesofeighty00cros/page/n9.

23. Sermon written by George Mathison, https://www.sermonwriter.com/hymn-stories/o-love-wilt-not-let-go/.

24. https://hymnary.org/person/Tullar_Grant.

For the first time, Jim and Elisabeth Elliot's daughter—Valerie Elliot Shepard—unseals the letters and private journals of her parents, capturing in first-person intimacy the attraction, struggle, drama, and devotion that became their most unlikely love story.

LEARN MORE *at* **DEVOTEDLYBOOK.COM**

DISCOVER
ELISABETH ELLIOT'S
MINISTRY, WRITING, & TEACHING

Now all in one place at

ElisabethElliot.org

The Elisabeth Elliot Foundation was created based on the life, love, and ministry of Elisabeth and Jim Elliot. Through the ElisabethElliot.org website and other media platforms, the Foundation brings together the writings and ministries of the Elliot Family in an evolving repository of their work, a resourceful collection of their writings and teachings, and a place to honor their legacy. It serves as an ongoing, worldwide outreach to help further the Foundation's mission to give:

Hope in Suffering
Restoration in Conflict
Joy in Obedience to the Lord Jesus Christ

Elisabeth Elliot
Foundation